Framework

RE

Joy White

3

Hodder Murray

A MEMBER OF THE HODDER HEADLINE GROUP

With special thanks to Brendan, Maddy Clark and Jane Tyler for their constant encouragement, support and most of all patience.

The Publishers would like to thank the following for permission to reproduce copyright material:

Photo credits p.3 *1* Corbis/Ashley Cooper, *2* Corbis/Narendra Shrestha/epa, *3* Getty Images/Magen David Adom (MDA), *4* Getty Images/Cris Bouroncle/AFP; **p.4** *5* Rex Features/Alix/Phanie, *6* Lorna Ainger; **p.7** *tl* Corbis/Eva-Lotta Jansson, *ml* Getty/Franco Origlia, *mr* Empics/Anwar Hussein, *br* Rex Features/SAE/Keystone USA; **p.8–9** Manchester Evening News; **p.10** ©The Singh Twins Amrit and Rabindra: www.singhtwins.co.uk; **p.12** *1* Corbis/Murat Taner/zefa, *2* Lorna Ainger, *3* Getty/Rob Elliott/AFP; **p.13** *4* Alamy/Robert Fried, *5* Alamy/World Religions Photo Library, *6* Corbis/Atef Hassan/Reuters, *7* Corbis/Kamal Kishore/Reuters; **p.14** Corbis/Bettmann; **p.15** Corbis/Lynn Goldsmith; **p.16–17** Matt Archer; **p.18** *l* Photofusion/Paula Glassman, *r* Corbis/David Rubinger; **p.24** Corbis/Vasily Fedosenko/Reuters; **p.25** *2* Joy White, *4* Corbis/Jeff J Mitchell/Reuters; **p.30** *bl* Liverpool Daily Post & Echo, *tr* Sefton Park Palm House Preservation Trust; **p.37** Empics/Fiona Hanson; **p.38** *1* Alamy/ArkReligion.com, *2* Courtesy Food for All, *3* Lorna Ainger; **p.39** *4* Still Pictures/Nic Dunlop/Christian Aid, *5* Photofusion/Joanne O'Brien; **p.40** *1* Corbis/Brecelj Bojan/Sygma, *2* Lorna Ainger; **p.41** *3* Lorna Ainger, *4* Joy White; **p.44** Corbis/Evelyn Hockstein/Reuters; **p.45** Corbis/Philippe Caron/Sygma; **p.46** *l & r* Alamy/Robert W. Ginn; **p.47** *tl* Corbis/Roman Soumar, *mr* Corbis/David Turnley, *b* Corbis/Jean Louis Atlan/Sygma; **p.50** *l* Corbis/Earl & Nazima Kowall, *r* NASA; **p.52** *t* Corbis/Bettmann, *b* Illustrated London News; **p.53** Corbis/Sion Touhig; **p.54** *1* Empics/Brennan Linsley/AP, *2* Getty Images/Robert Sullivan/AFP; **p.55** *3* Alamy/Doug Steley, *4* Photodisc, *5* Rex Features/Vesa Moilanen; **p.58** *1* Getty Images/Romeo Gacad, *2* Alamy/Fotosonline, *3* Corbis/Ajay Verma/Reuters; **p.59** *4* Corbis/Jose L. Pelaez, *5* World Religions Photo Library/Sagatowski, *6* Alamy/Stock Connection Distribution, *7* Getty Images/Toshifumi Kitamura; **p.60** *tl* Alamy/Barry Lewis, *tr* Alamy/Dinodia Images, *ml* Corbis, *mr* Corbis/Gideon Mendel, *br* Photodisc; **p.61** Alamy/ArkReligion.com; **p.62** *bl* AKG-Images, *tr* Alamy/ArkReligion.com, *br* Corbis/Stephen Hird/Reuters; **p.63** *tl* Getty Images/Julian Herbert, *br* Getty Images/Stephen Dunn; **p.64** *tr* World Religions Photo Library/Christine Osborne, *bl* Alamy/ArkReligion.com, *br* Alamy/ArkReligion.com; **p.65** Getty Images/Narinder Nanu; **p.66–7** AKG-Images; **p.68** From The Bhaktivedanta Book Trust Int'l ©2006; **p.75** Corbis/Bettmann; **p.77** *tl* Courtesy Native Energy, *r* Corbis/Andreu Dalmau/epa, *b* Logo reproduced with kind permission of The Body Shop International plc.; **p.78** *tr* Lorna Ainger, *bl* Empics/Martin Rickett/PA; **p.79** Corbis/Neal Preston; **p.80** *1* Photodisc, *2* Alamy/Photofusion, *3* Getty Images/Jeff Vanuga/USDA Natural Resources Conservation Service, *4* Photodisc; **p.81** *5* Rex Features, *6* Photodisc, *7* Corbis/Alessandro della Bella/epa, *8* Corbis/Ashley Cooper; **p.82** Corbis/London Aerial Photo Library; **p.83** Corbis/John McAnulty; **p.86** Getty Images/Paula Bronstein; **p.87** *t* Courtesy Bhaktivedanta Manor, *b* Courtesy Islamic Foundation for Ecology and Environmental Sciences;

p.88 Corbis/Reuters; **p.90 & p.91** *t & b* Corbis/David Turnley; **p.93** Corbis/Juda Ngwenya/Reuters; **p.96** Empics/Oded Balilty/AP; **p.97** Corbis/National Gallery Collection, by kind permission of the Trustees of the National Gallery, London; **p.100** *1* Corbis/Kai Pfaffenbach/Reuters, *2* Getty/Stephen Jaffe/AFP; **p.102** ©Judy Cunningham Van Hoy; **p.103** *t* Corbis/Chris Helgren/Reuters, *b* ©Coventry Cathedral/Josefina De Vasconcellos; **p.106** *t* Corbis/Louise Gubb, *b* Getty Images/Tauseef Mustafa; **p.107** *t* Courtesy of Art Miles Project, *b* Getty Images/Koichi Kamoshida; **p.108** Corbis/Reinhard Krause/Reuters; **p.109** Martin Melaugh; **p.110** Courtesy Children of Abraham Project; **p.111** *t, m & b* Community Spirit; **p.112** *l, m & r* Courtesy Tariq Khamisa Foundation; **p.113** Courtesy Tariq Khamisa Foundation; **p.115** L'Chayim USA; **p.117** *t* Empics/Gene Herrick/AP, *b* Corbis/Bettmann; **p.118** *t* Courtesy Visas for Life Foundation, *b* Joy White; **p.119** Getty Images/Hector Mata/AFP.

Acknowledgements p.16–17 Matthew Archer and Open House www.mkarcher.com; **p.30** Liverpool Community Spirit for accounts from *Altaring Liverpool*; **p.116** 'It isn't right to fight'© John Foster 1995 from *Standing on the Sidelines* (Oxford University Press) included by permission of the author.

The publishers would also like to thank the following:

Muhammad Ali; British Humanist Association; Ebury Press & Alzheimers Disease Society (Jonathan Sachs quote); Hodder (scripture quotations taken from the HOLY BIBLE, NEW INTERNATIONAL VERSION. Copyright © 1973, 1978, 1984 by International Bible Society. Used by permission of Hodder & Stoughton Publishers, A member of the Hodder Headline Group. All rights reserved. "NIV" is a registered trademark of International Bible Society. UK trademark number 1448790.); Martin Luther King; Reader's Digest (three extracts from 'What Guides My Life'); Labi Siffre (So Strong); Swami Vivekananda; WellBeing (three extracts from 'My Well-being').

Every effort has been made to trace all copyright holders, but if any have been inadvertently overlooked the Publishers will be pleased to make the necessary arrangements at the first opportunity.

Although every effort has been made to ensure that website addresses are correct at time of going to press, Hodder Murray cannot be held responsible for the content of any website mentioned in this book. It is sometimes possible to find a relocated web page by typing in the address of the home page for a website in the URL window of your browser.

Orders: please contact Bookpoint Ltd, 130 Milton Park, Abingdon, Oxon OX14 4SB. Telephone: (44) 01235 827720. Fax: (44) 01235 400454. Lines are open from 9.00–5.00, Monday to Saturday, with a 24-hour message answering service. Visit our website at www.hoddereducation.co.uk.

Cover photo: Photograph of hands by John Lund/Corbis
Typeset in 11pt Formata Light by Black Dog Design
Internal illustrations by Daedalus Studios (cartoons) and Barking Dog Art
Printed in Italy

A catalogue record for this title is available from the British Library

ISBN-10: 0 340 90410 0

ISBN-13: 978 0340 90410 7

Contents

UNIT 1: HOW DOES RELIGION MATTER?

Lesson 1: Why do I need to know about religions?

◎ Consider the impact of different religions.

◎ Express ideas about possible consequences of belonging to a religion.

◎ Identify the different careers that need an understanding of different religions.

Lesson 2: What is the impact of religion in the world?

◎ Identify features of religion in the local community.

◎ Consider the impact of religion on a range of current issues.

◎ Evaluate the challenges and tensions of belonging to a religion.

Lesson 3: What impact can religion have on the individual?

◎ Consider the different features of our own identities.

◎ Find out about how religion can affect someone from birth to death.

◎ Learn about the impact of Islam on one individual.

Lesson 4: How can a religion give purpose to life?

◎ Think about the purpose of life.

◎ Learn about Christian views on vocation.

◎ Find out about the work of Open House.

◎ Distinguish between having a vocation and doing a job.

Lesson 5: How might believers in the same religion differ?

◎ Think about how believers in the same religion will have different beliefs and practices.

◎ Consider why it is wrong to use stereotypes.

◎ Learn about some of the different practices between Orthodox and Reform Jews.

Lesson 6: What are people's rights regarding religion?

◎ Consider what it means to practise a religion.

◎ Find out about the role of religion in China.

◎ Consider some of the challenges of practising a religion.

◎ Identify the effects of prejudice and discrimination.

1. Why do I need to know about religions?

SKILLS

- **identifying the impact** of religion on the individual, within the community and globally
  - **expressing ideas** about possible consequences of belonging to a religion
  - **recognising** the different careers that need a knowledge and understanding of religions

ACTIVITY ONE ....

Look carefully at pictures 1–6 here and on page 4. Each is an example of the impact of religion or beliefs either on the individual, within the community or within the world.

For each picture choose two captions from the lists below (a–f and i–iv) to explain the impact of religion.

When I was fourteen Sunday was the day of rest. Everyone in our street went to church. Shops weren't open and you couldn't even hang out your washing. Things have changed. Religion used to be such a part of everyone's life.

Is this the way you would describe Sunday?

Does the fact that fewer people attend church in Britain than in the past mean that people are less religious? What role does religion play in:

- our lives
- our **community**
- our world?

We only have to walk down the street, turn on the TV, go to the cinema or surf the Internet to realise that whether we are religious or not the **impact** of religion affects us all personally, within our community and within our world.

Captions

First match a caption from this list, then one from the second list (i–vi) below:

a) Many people wear something special to show they belong to a religious tradition.

b) Religions often give answers to important questions, like, 'What will happen when I die?'

c) Many religions have charities in Britain and overseas which work locally with people to help them.

d) People of different religions send aid at times of disaster.

e) Many religions teach the importance of care for animals.

f) Some people consider it important to be educated in faith schools.

i) For example, Israeli aid is put together in Tel Aviv, to be sent to New Orleans to help people affected by Hurricane Katrina.

ii) For example, many Sikh males will wear a turban.

iii) For example, Islamic Relief staff provide long- and short-term aid to displaced Sudanese people in an encampment in Western Dafur, Africa.

iv) For example, many Christians believe that the soul goes to heaven.

v) For example, Hindus show respect to the cow and will usually not eat beef.

vi) For example, in many local communities pupils can attend Anglican and Catholic schools.

1

2

3

4

5

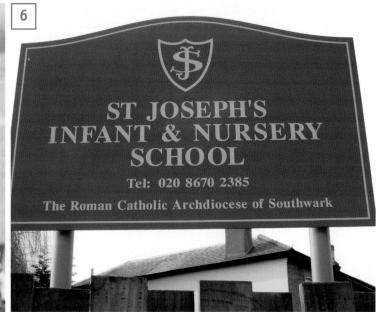

6

When someone has a religious belief it often has an impact on many parts of their life and on the lives of the people around them.

ACTIVITY TWO ••

Set out a table like the one below. For each picture 1–6 decide if you think it is having an impact on a person, a community or the world, and put a tick in the correct column. Remember some pictures may fit into more than one category. Be ready to justify your reasons.

Picture	Personal	Community	Global
1			
2			
3			
4			
5			
6			

Whether we are religious or not, we live in a world where we need to know about people's religions and the way they affect what believers do, wear, eat, how they behave and the choices that they make. Many companies now run courses for their employees where they are taught about religious practices.

FLEXIBLE FAITH

Leading companies have pledged to extend flexible working to help employees celebrate holy days. Firms including the BBC and Shell also announced plans to set up prayer rooms in the workplace. Carole Waters of BT said understanding faith was 'essential to business'.

Daily Post

ACTIVITY THREE ·············

1. Read the extract 'Flexible Faith' above right. Then for each of the areas (a–c) draw a spider diagram as shown below. Complete each diagram by listing two jobs where it would be 'essential to business' to know a person's religion and explain why. One example has been done for you.

   a) What people eat.

   b) Which are the religious festivals.

   c) What happens when someone dies.

2. With a partner identify some situations or times in a person's life when they would be asked which religion they belong to, for example when being admitted into a hospital.

NOW TRY THIS ···········

Think about a career that you would like to follow.

Consider how a knowledge and understanding of religious beliefs would help you deal with any people you might meet in the job. For example:

A job I would be interested in doing is ...

It would help me know and understand people's religions because ...

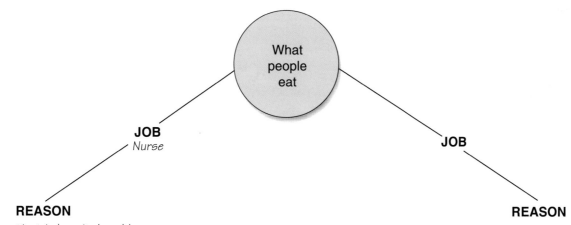

2. What is the impact of religion in the world?

SKILLS

- **finding** features of religion in the local community
- **investigating** the impact of religion on current issues
- **evaluating** the challenges and tensions of belonging to a religion

ACTIVITY ONE ....

Look at the picture below for three minutes and then close your book. With a partner write down what you can remember from the picture. How many items on your list are connected to religious beliefs or practices?

The first lesson helped you to understand why, on a personal level, we need to learn about the different beliefs and practices people have.

Religious Education also helps us to make sense of the world we live in. Whether we are religious or not we need to have a knowledge and understanding of religions to make sense of the community and world we live in.

Every day we read in newspapers how religion affects or is affected by all that is going on in the world. What we learn about in Religious Education helps us to make sense of the events and to form opinions.

ACTIVITY TWO

Select one of the newspaper headlines. Write five bullet points of information that you think might appear in the article.

Headscarves ban – girl pupil sent home for wearing the <u>hijab</u>

'I became a churchgoer so my son could go to a Church School'

Pope Says No To Use of Condoms

Prince Charles Visits Local <u>Gurdwara</u>

New Kosher Restaurant will help Jewish Community

GOLDA'S KOSHER RESTAURANT

Church helps local refugee family

▲ *Why do you think a statue of Jesus was placed in a clothes shop? Do you know any other examples when advertising has offended people?*

A clothing store in Manchester has received many complaints concerning the statue it has placed in the middle of the shop window. The statue is a large representation of Jesus and is surrounded by a range of clothes. The shop is very near to a number of places of worship including churches and **mosques**. Helen Whittaker, 16, said, 'I wouldn't call myself religious but I know a lot of people who are upset. To be honest it doesn't bother me but I don't know why it is in the shop window. It wouldn't make me go and buy my jeans from the shop.'

ACTIVITY THREE ....

Imagine you have been asked by the manager of the shop to help with the situation in the account described above. The people who work at the shop have raised a number of questions that they want you to answer.

- Why have people complained?
- Who does it affect?
- What should we do next?

NOW TRY THIS ....

How would you reply to the following view?

> I never talk about religion when I'm with people I don't know – you never know what people think.

KEY WORDS

Gurdwara   the Sikh place of worship

Hijab   modest dress worn by many Muslim women to cover their hair and bodies

Mosque   the Muslim place of worship

3. What impact can religion have on the individual?

SKILLS

- **reflecting upon** the different features of your own identity
- **recognising** that religion is an important part of many people's identities
- **investigating** the impact of belonging to a religion for the individual
- **recognising** the role of free will and free choice

Our **identity** is made up of many different parts.

Often it will include:

- the influence of our family and friends
- where we were born
- what important things have happened to us
- the traditions we follow
- the beliefs we have.

For each person this will be a unique combination.

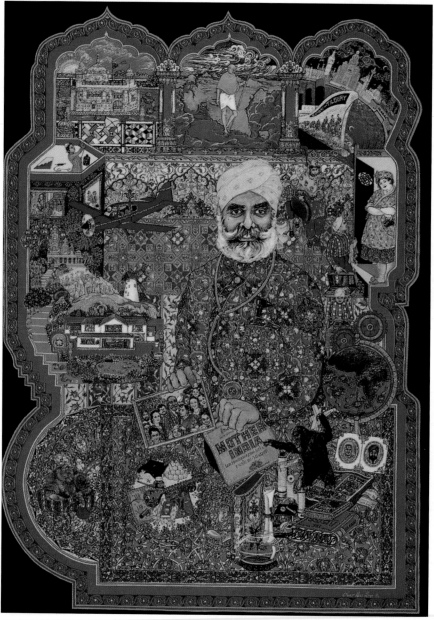

All that I am,
by Amrit KD Kaur Singh.

ACTIVITY ONE ....

1. Look at the picture. It is called *All That I Am* by a Sikh artist called Amrit KD Kaur Singh and is a personal tribute to her father. It represents experiences and influences on her father's life which made him the person he is.

   Start your observation in the left-hand corner and with a partner identify:

   a) what experiences he has had in his life

   b) what he considers important.

2. The picture also shows the impact the father has had on his daughter, the artist. Reflect on and write down what values and experiences you think have become a part of your identity because of your family experiences.

For many people their religious beliefs and the religious **tradition** they follow will have an effect from birth until death.

What is important in their lives?

Will they have a religious ceremony when they are born?

As they become a teenager will they confirm their faith perhaps through a ceremony?

What moral decisions will they make?

Who will they marry?

However, although many people are born into a religious tradition, it doesn't always mean they will stay a practising member of that religion. There could be a time in their life when they make the decision for themselves.

ACTIVITY TWO •••••••••••••••

Adel is a Muslim who was born in London but now lives in Norfolk. Throughout his life his belief in Islam has been very important.

1. Look at pictures 1–7 of events that might take place during a Muslim's life. Read captions a–g of Adel's life below. Decide which caption matches which picture.

2. Write down the order in which you think these pictures would take place in Adel's life.

3. With a partner identify which of the pictures might happen just once in Adel's life.

4. For each of the pictures identify which you think would be the major influences:

   a) Adel's conscience

   b) Adel's family

   c) Adel's friends

   d) religious teachings.

Captions

a) Whispering the **adhan** into Adel's ear when he is born to welcome him into the **Ummah**.

b) Celebrating **Id-ul-Fitr**.

c) Learning the whole of the Qur'an by heart to become a **hafiz**.

d) Being wrapped in white and circumcised (Khitan) to fulfil the command of Allah to the prophet **Ibrahim**.

e) Deciding whether to eat halal (allowed) food.

f) Deciding who to marry.

g) Considering the big questions of life such as why do people suffer; what happens after you die?

KEY WORDS

Adhan   the call to prayer

Hafiz   title given to Muslims who learn the whole of the Qur'an by heart

Id-ul-Fitr   Muslim festival marking the end of Ramadan, the month of fasting

Ummah   the worldwide community of Muslims

3

6

4

7

For all of us there will be parts of our own family or community identity that will be passed on from one generation to another.

'More than most Jews have reflected on the power of memory to shape identity. The Hebrew Bible is full of commands to remember. We carry our past with us, and it helps to make us who we are.'

(The Chief Rabbi for Jews in Britain, Jonathan Sachs)

5

NOW TRY THIS ....

Read the quote from Jonathan Sachs above.

Reflect upon what aspects of your past you carry with you, which help to make you who you are.

4. How can a religion give purpose to life?

> ## SKILLS
> - **reflecting upon** your own views concerning the purpose of life
> - **understanding** Christian views on vocation
> - **investigating** the impact of religious beliefs through a life story

A traditional Jewish story tells of a young man who had three dreams when he left home:

- *to be famous*

- *to own a Rolls-Royce*

- *to marry a beautiful woman.*

By the age of 30 he had done all three. So was he happy then?
No, he grew more and more depressed – what was there for him to do with the rest of his life?

▲ **Martin Luther King was a Baptist Minister who led a campaign to end the segregation laws in Alabama.**

Many people have a goal in life. They want their lives to count in some way and to matter even after they have died.

The American Civil Rights Leader Martin Luther King once said:

> *'I am convinced that it is not the fear of death that haunts our sleep so much as the fear that our lives will not have mattered, that as far as the world is concerned, we might as well never have lived. What we miss in our lives, no matter how much we have, is that sense of meaning.'*

(Martin Luther King)

ACTIVITY ONE ●●●●●●●●●●●●●●●

1. Consider the list below. Put it into order, with what would give you most purpose in life at the top, and what would give you least purpose at the bottom.

   a) Winning a reality TV show, e.g. *Big Brother*.

   b) Being a millionaire by the time you are 30.

   c) Writing a best-selling book.

   d) Inventing a cure for cancer.

   e) Helping and caring for all your family.

   f) Scoring the winning goal in the World Cup.

2. Imagine you could be remembered for one thing after your death. What would you like to be remembered for? Why?

In the last lesson we saw the role that religion played for Adel from his birth to his death. For many people, having a religion gives them a sense of purpose in life and it can also affect their actions.

Olympic gold medal-winning boxer Cassius Clay reverted to Islam and changed his name to Muhammad Ali. Because of his religious beliefs he refused to join the US army and fight in the Vietnam War (1963–75). As a result, the US government did not allow him to box for three years and deprived him of his world heavyweight championship title and medals.

Look At All The Buildings

Look at all the buildings in downtown New York

People built them

They're dead now

But the buildings are still standing

We don't own anything: but we're just trustees,

Think about it!

We're all going to die.

This life is a test.

Try and pass the test.

I'm trying, and I'm going to make it to heaven.

That's the eternal life.

By Muhammad Ali

ACTIVITY TWO ●●●●●●●●●●●●●

From the poem how do you think Muhammad Ali would view material objects and possessions?

◀ *Muhammad Ali's beliefs would not allow him to fight in the Vietnam War. What else do you know about Muhammad Ali?*

15

Some people believe their religion gives them a sense of purpose and tells them what is important to do with their lives. This can include the job they choose or feel they are driven to do.

Christians believe that God has a purpose for each individual and that this includes a use of their talents. Some Christians consider that work is a duty to God and that they are called by God to do a particular job. This is known as a **vocation** and comes from the Latin 'vocare' meaning 'to call'. Many people believe that God calls men and women to serve him through their work.

One person who believes this is Matthew Archer who gave up a job teaching in England to work with street children in Brazil.

Where do you work?

I work in Open House which provides a shelter for homeless children in Brazil. A place where children can wash and get clean clothes and a meal. We also run a programme of games and education.

▲ *Homeless Brazilian children eating food provided by Open House.*

Why didn't you choose to help people in England?

I have helped people in England but think there are greater needs in other parts of the world. When I saw so many children living on the streets in Brazil I decided to stay and try to make a difference.

Were you ever afraid?

I often get afraid when the street children fight each other. They can change personality very quickly, and become extremely violent and dangerous.

How is your work making a difference?

In Open House children are educated socially and spiritually, as well as academically. They learn how to wash themselves, to eat, and to sleep at a normal time of day. They learn how to solve disputes without violence. Most importantly they learn how to value themselves and others around them.

▲ *Matthew Archer with his wife, Karina.*

Where is God in all this?

I believe that God is in the centre of everything we do. I believe it was God who called me and I had the faith to follow.

ACTIVITY THREE..............

1. Read the interview with Matthew. Copy and complete the **concept map** below giving details of how Matthew has shown courage, service and faith through his vocation to work in Open House.

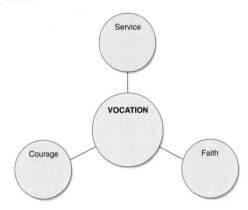

2. To another question Matthew answered:

   'To follow God's commands and to do His will. It is different for everyone but in my case it is to rescue, serve, care for and educate needy children.'

   What do you think the question was?

3. You have been asked to complete the interview with Matthew. Which three of the questions listed below would you select to give you a greater understanding about Matthew's vocation?

   a) How often do you go back to England?

   b) What do your friends and family think of what you do?

   c) Do you pray?

   d) If God is good why are there homeless people?

   e) Have you always been a Christian?

   f) Why is your centre called Open House?

NOW TRY THIS ....

Explain to your partner in less than twenty words the difference between doing a job and having a vocation.

5. How might believers in the same religion differ?

Think of your class. You are a community and have a lot in common such as living in the same area, being the same age and going to the same school. But you also have many individual features.

Just as in your class, within a religious tradition there will be a wide range of different beliefs, practices and traditions.

Although Judaism is one of the smallest religions with just over 17 million Jews spread throughout many parts of the world, like all religions there is a wide range of different beliefs, practices and traditions.

ACTIVITY ONE

1. Use the words 'few', 'some', 'all' or 'many' to complete these sentences.

   a) … pupils in this class are learning Religious Education.

   b) … pupils in this class are vegetarians.

   c) … pupils in this class like *Coronation Street*.

   d) … pupils in this class believe it is wrong to go to war.

   e) … pupils in this class celebrate Christmas.

2. It would be wrong to **stereotype** you as a group as if you all believed in one thing or behaved in the same way. Why do you think it is wrong and harmful to use stereotypes when referring to people who believe in the same religion?

▲ *An Orthodox Jew, wearing phylacteries (parchment with passages of scripture written on them) on his arm and forehead.*

▲ *Reform Jew, Rabbi Naamah Kelman.*

Some Jews hold few, if any, religious beliefs but they are still Jewish because they were born Jewish. These people are called **secular Jews**. Other Jews believe they should live their lives as close to the rules laid down in the **Torah** as possible. These are called **Orthodox Jews**. Followers of **Reform Judaism** believe that the Jewish religion should interpret the Torah to reflect the times. There are many different types of Jews, just as there are different types of Hindus or Christians.

Being Jewish doesn't stop a person being Chinese, Indian, English, Welsh or American – that is their nationality and will also have an effect on the customs and traditions they follow. Within any community you may find people who are Jewish but who practise their religion in different ways.

ACTIVITY TWO ....

Draw two overlapping circles like the ones shown here. Label one Orthodox and the other Reform. Read Leah and Jo's conversation below and put into the circles anything distinctive about Orthodox and Reform Jews. Where the circles overlap write anything that is a shared practice or belief.

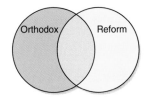

Jo *Have you met Rebecca – the new girl in year 10? We went out with her last night and she refused to eat anything at all. I know she's Jewish but when you come out with us you eat all sorts of food.*

Leah *Perhaps she's an Orthodox Jew.*

Jo *I don't understand! Does that mean she eats special Jewish food?*

Leah *No! There is no such thing as Jewish food! There are certain foods that many Jews cannot eat or mix together. We don't all follow the rules in exactly the same way. Sometimes it depends upon the country that our grandparents have come from. It's like an American Christian might be more likely to eat hamburgers and an Indian Christian a rice dish. At our synagogue we had a Nigerian Jew come to visit us and they have banana wine for their Friday night* **Kiddush** *wine.*

If she is an Orthodox Jew then she will follow all the laws that are set down in the Torah. That's the ...

Jo *I know what that is. I do listen in R.E. It's the first five books of the Bible. So it's the Orthodox who are the old-fashioned ones.*

Leah *They aren't at all. That's the way that R.E. books often stereotype them.*

What's distinctive is the way that they consider the sacred texts. Take food, for example. In my family we only eat animals that are declared **kosher***, or fit, like lamb or beef or*

chicken and the fish we eat must have fins and scales. Before we eat the meat it must have been prepared following kosher rules, so it is killed and prepared in a certain way. We also don't mix meat and milk at the same meal. My uncle is an Orthodox Jew and he considers it really important to keep all the kosher rules. On flights if there is no kosher provision he won't eat as he doesn't know if the food has been prepared in a kitchen where meat and milk dishes have been mixed. Orthodox Jews can only eat in places where food laws are strictly followed.

Jo *So you share the same beliefs but you practise them in different ways.*

Leah *Yes. It's the same with* **Shabbat***. We consider it very special too but we believe that modern conveniences, for example, electricity, cars, etc., enhance Shabbat rest and holiness. So we will drive to the synagogue and we do use electricity.*

Jo *But won't you be punished for not keeping the law?*

Leah *Punished by who? God? My family believes God gave us free will to make the decision. I don't believe it makes me less of a Jew. Do you remember what Gurpal said in RE last week?*

Jo *Yes, he got really mad when Miss said that all Sikhs wear a turban. He explained that it's his beliefs and practices that make him a Sikh, not whether he wears a turban or not.*

ACTIVITY THREE ....

1. You are doing a study exchange and have just found out that the person staying with you is Jewish and follows a Kosher lifestyle. You need to plan how you will find out more information and where you can get the appropriate foods locally.

   With a partner construct a plan showing how you could refer to:

   a) websites – list three websites
      that might help you

   b) books – name three books
      that might help you

   c) asking – identify two people who might
      give you information.

2. Which do you think would be the most reliable source of evidence? Be prepared to justify your decision to your partner.

3. Are there any other sources of information you could refer to?

ACTIVITY FOUR ••••••••••••••••••••••••••••••••••••

How would you respond to the following statements?

a)

All Jews are the same.

b)

All Jews look the same.

c)

Only a true Jew eats kosher food.

d)

She can't be Jewish, she's from India.

e)

That restaurant sells Jewish food.

NOW TRY THIS •••••••••••

Consider the following view and write one argument against it and one to support it.

'If you are really religious then you should obey all the rules in the same way.'

I agree because ...

I disagree because ...

(Remember to use evidence to support each argument.)

KEY WORDS

Kiddush   a prayer usually recited over wine at Shabbat (see below) and other festivals

Kosher   foods or practices that are allowed for Jews

Orthodox Judaism   a form of Judaism believing in the traditional teachings of the religion

Reform Judaism   a form of Judaism believing that all the old laws of Judaism do not have to be followed exactly

Secular Jew   Jews who do not normally consider religion as important but have been born of a Jewish mother

Shabbat   Jewish holy day (Sabbath) beginning at Friday sunset and ending on Saturday at nightfall

Stereotype   a person or thing considered to represent a group

Torah   the Jewish holy scripture

6. What are people's rights regarding religion?

The human **right** to practise a religion is stated within the Universal Declaration of Human Rights and the United Nations Rights for Every Child.

'Everyone has the right to freedom of thought, conscience and religion and the right to express their opinion both privately and publicly.'

'All children have the right to think and believe what they want and to practice their religion.'

Throughout the world, some people find it difficult to exercise their rights without fear of **discrimination** or punishment. Although freedom to exercise religion is a part of the Universal Declaration of Human Rights there are many incidents reported by **Amnesty International** of abuse throughout the world. More Christians have been killed because of their religion in the twentieth century than in the previous nine centuries combined.

ACTIVITY ONE

There are many views about what the essential parts of 'practising' a religion are. Draw the template of the circles below and with a partner select, from the list (1–10), which you think religious people should have a right to and place the numbers in the circles to show how important you think they are.

1. Read their sacred text at home.
2. Wear clothes or symbols without being abused.
3. Worship at a place of worship.
4. Have festival days off from school.
5. Speak about their religion to other people.
6. Go to a school where everyone follows their religion.
7. Have equal rights when applying for any job.
8. Learn about their religion at school.
9. Worship in places of worship that are free from graffiti.
10. Not to be bullied or abused because of their religion.

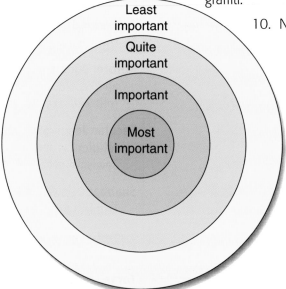

Least important
Quite important
Important
Most important

In some countries there is a history of **persecuting** people because of their religion. For example:

1. In China, the government administers five recognised religions (Buddhism, Taoism, Islam, Protestantism and Catholicism). People who worship can only do so at state-sanctioned places of worship.

   Zhiang Rongliang is the leader of the China for Christ Church – one of the largest 'house churches'. So far he has been imprisoned five times for his beliefs, for a total of twelve years, during which he has been severely tortured.

2. In Britain the Community Security Trust (which protects synagogues and Jewish places of interest) reports a rise in **anti-Semitism** and acts of discrimination. These have included arson attacks, attacks on graves and attacks on people.

3. In the same way newspapers report a rise in **Islamaphobia**, especially since 11 September 2001, with one in three Muslims in Britain having suffered abuse.

Often newspapers will carry reports of the attacks but they don't always tell the whole story. Look at the following two accounts of an attack on a local mosque.

Saliha's account

When my father and brother came back from their **Maghrib prayers** they were shaking. My father wouldn't talk about it but my brother was really angry. They had just begun their prayers when suddenly stones started to be thrown through the windows. The shattered glass fell on some of the young children who were sitting by the windows. When my brother ran to the door he found that a pig's head had been nailed on the mosque and graffiti had been sprayed all over the walls. The cowards had run away. How could they do this? Do they realise how scared they have made us feel? The mosque is our place of safety and a focus for all the community and now it has been defiled.

Local Mosque Damaged

On Thursday night, the mosque in Pevsham was attacked by a group of young people. The Imam reported that no one was hurt although windows were broken.

Daily Post

KEY WORDS

Anti-Semitism hostility to or against Jews

Islamaphobia irrational fear or dislike of Muslims

Maghrib prayer compulsory daytime prayer for Muslims

ACTIVITY TWO

1. Make a list of the further information given by Saliha's account which is not in the newspaper account.

2. Compare the accounts and decide which is the more reliable evidence for what happened.

ACTIVITY THREE ••

1. Look at the pictures and speech bubble 1–4 below and opposite. Draw a table like the one below and categorise them under the correct heading. Some may go under more than one heading.

Prejudice – prejudging	Attacks on person	Attacks on places

2. You are a reporter working on a local paper and have been asked to cover a story related to one of the images of persecution. Your brief will be to talk to relevant people. You need to:

a) explain why you have chosen this story

b) decide who you will talk to, to find out the facts

c) write a list of the questions you will ask them.

◀ *This Jewish grave has had graffiti sprayed onto it. What should happen to the people who do this? Why would the graffiti shock any relatives visiting the grave?*

NOW TRY THIS ••••••••••••

Why do you think someone continues to practise a religion even when they are going to be punished for it?

2

3

I never mix with them they wear strange clothes don't they?

◄ *This security van is parked outside the synagogue so that the building and worshippers aren't attacked.*

4

▲ *Anwar-E-Madina Mosque in Edinburgh after an arson attack. Who do you think would be affected by this?*

25

SUMMARY OF UNIT 1

Lesson 2

You have learned that religion has an impact on many current issues.

Lesson 3

You have learned that religion can have an effect on people from birth to death.

Lesson 1

You have learned that religion has an impact on individuals and communities.

How does religion matter?

Lesson 4

You have learned that religion can give a purpose to some people's lives.

Lesson 6

You have learned about people's rights, and some challenges of belonging to a religion.

Lesson 5

You have learned that believers in the same religion may have different beliefs and practices.

UNIT 2: WHAT IS THE IMPACT OF DIFFERENT RELIGIONS ON THE COMMUNITY?

Lesson 1: Why are communities important?

◎ Identify the communities we belong to.

◎ Reflect upon the role of the community in people's lives.

◎ Learn about religious communities.

Lesson 2: Why do people help others in the community?

◎ Think about the different ways we can serve a community.

◎ Read about Buddhist, Christian, Hindu, Humanist, Muslim, Jewish and Sikh beliefs concerning service.

◎ Consider examples of personal sacrifice.

Lesson 3: What role do religions play in the community?

◎ Learn about how different religions serve the community.

◎ Read about how Faithworks serves the community.

◎ Consider if religions should get involved in the community.

Lesson 4: Why are there different types of schools?

◎ Identify different types of faith schools.

◎ Think about the arguments for and against faith schools.

◎ Decide for yourself if there should be faith schools within your community by considering different arguments.

Lesson 5: Why do some religious communities live apart?

◎ Discover why some people choose to live in monasteries and convents.

◎ Think about the meaning of poverty, chastity and obedience.

◎ Learn about the way of life for the Amish.

What is the impact of different religions on the community?

1. Why are communities important?

SKILLS

- **defining and applying** the concept of community
  - **recognising** the importance for many people of belonging to a faith community
  - **expressing insights** into your own and others' views on the importance of belonging

ACTIVITY ONE ....

1. Make a list of the communities you belong to. The pictures below and opposite should help you think of some but there may be others.

   Now share your list with a partner and see if you have forgotten any.

2. Draw a table like the one below and answer the questions for four of the communities you belong to.

Type of community	
a) Do you have to be a certain age to enter and leave?	
b) Do you wear special clothes or symbols of identity?	
c) What is the common purpose of the community?	
d) How do you celebrate together as a community?	

Within your community there will be many places which will have a special significance throughout your life. 'Altaring Liverpool' was a project undertaken where 100 people from a local community were asked to identify an area that was of deep value or **sacred** to them and to place an altar there.

A wide range of places were selected with different reasons but all made reference to the importance of belonging to a community and a feeling of **awe** in a particular place. Even if people hadn't been to that place for a number of years they could still remember that particular feeling of **wonder** and **reverence**.

'Fifty-nine Catherine Street is where I grew up as a child and it is also where our daughter, Aliyah – who passed away on 2 July 2001 – was born. It has a lot of fond memories for us and some bad ones. But the good times outweigh the bad. At the top of the house, we feel like we are getting closer to God.'

▼ **'Sefton Park is the place I go to meditate in quiet contemplation. The park has many sides to it like a many-sided diamond. It's a beautiful place to be and I always take my friends there for a stroll. It reminds me to check myself when my mind gets too hectic, to not take things seriously, and that, at the end of the day, taking the time to get back in touch with Mother Nature is what makes life such a delight.'**

'I chose the Al-Ghazali Centre because we live in a community where everyone is striving for the same thing – unity, justice and peace. Over twenty staff and volunteers work at the centre on all sorts of different projects with people of different ages and backgrounds. In this, my work place, I feel that everyone is reaching for the same goals and working together and I think that this has a very positive impact both on my community and myself.'

◀ **'The Law Centre is a very special place for me and my family. It was my husband Rashid and other people of the community who set it up. Every time I pass the building, I feel pride but also great pain thinking of our loss. It is a living memory of the turbulent times we lived through, the struggles and pains friends and colleagues endured. The Law Centre is a place of hope and pride, a place where people of all nations can get support, help and education.'**

ACTIVITY TWO ....

1. Copy and complete the concept map below to show why the people chose the places described on page 30.

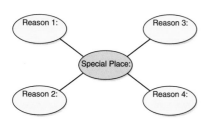

2. Describe a place to your partner where you feel a sense of awe and reverence.

Many people in the 'Altaring Liverpool' project referred to various places of worship in the community. For people of all religious traditions the worshipping community is extremely important. Believers may meet with their faith communities locally or they may have to travel a long distance.

ACTIVITY THREE ....

Look at the quotes on this page from people who live in the same community – all gain something extra by belonging to their own religious community. Decide which quote is an example of each of the following benefits of belonging to a religious community. (Each quote may reveal more than one benefit.)

1. Meeting people.
2. Giving a source of hope.
3. Learning about a religion.
4. Giving a feeling of belonging.
5. Giving a sense of identity.
6. Sharing beliefs.
7. Sharing cultural activities.

a) When I go to the mandir I meet people who celebrate my festivals. This is important as it's hard to get excited about Divali when there are no other Hindus around me of my age.

Vijay

b) Going to the mosque makes me realise what is important. I feel part of a group of people all working together for one cause – it might be to support charities like Islamic Relief or to hold interfaith evenings so people can understand more about Islam.

Adel

c) dI am the only Sikh in my school. By going to the gurdwara I feel part of a community where we celebrate the same events.

Parminder

d) When I first came to the country I felt really accepted when I went to church. They helped me with so many practical and spiritual things.

Leon

e) It's important for me to attend Shul or synagogue. Although I have moved away from the area I go back there each Saturday. It's where my grandfather went and my father. I feel it's touching my roots.

Rebekah

f) I go to mosque school after school. It helps me learn Arabic and about my religion. All my brothers and cousins go.

Nasima

g) I attend an Alpha course which helps me learn more about Christianity. Although I am always tired when I go it always makes me feel more energetic when I leave.

Leah

h) When my sister was so ill it meant such a lot to hear that the community were praying for her.

Fran

NOW TRY THIS ....

You have been asked to explain the term 'community' to eight-year-old children in your local primary school. Either draw a logo/diagram or write a description.

2. Why do people help others in the community?

4

5

ACTIVITY ONE ....

1. With a partner decide what order you think the pictures happened in.

2. If you had to give a title that summed up the message of the pictures what would you decide?

We have all heard of rich people having servants who are paid to do jobs such as cooking or cleaning. Many people in today's society consider it important to serve others in the community without any form of payment. They sacrifice their own time or money. Often the people who they serve are those who are in need of support.

Many people consider service is love in action and is the greatest gift a human being can give to another. By doing this someone may need to make a personal sacrifice of time, money or even their lives.

ACTIVITY TWO ....

1. Copy the line below and decide where on the line you would place the following:

   a) Caring

   b) Loving

   c) Noticing

   d) Serving

   e) Respecting.

   Shows least love in action ⟷ Shows greatest love in action

2. At each end of the line write or draw an example of what the concept means in practice, for example, I show I care for my dog by feeding him and taking him out for his walks.

Buddhism

Buddhism teaches that people should show compassion for all beings. According to the Dhammapada, serving those in need is not a burden but sweetness. It is an opportunity to share happiness and do something good before leaving this life.

'To have friends in need is sweet
And to share happiness,
And to have done something good
Before leaving this life is sweet.'

(Dhammapada 23)

Humanism

Humanists believe that communities can work well and increase happiness by caring for young and old and treating others in a way you would want to be treated.

'Treat other people as you would want to be
treated in their situation; do not do things you
would not want to have done to you.'

(British Humanist Association, 1999)

Judaism

Judaism teaches that everyone is responsible for each other. Those who do not perform kind acts do not know God.

'All men are responsible for one another.
Even a poor man who himself subsists on
charity should give charity.
He who prays for his fellowman,
While he himself has the same need,
Will be answered first.'

(Sanhedrin 27a)

Christianity

Christian scriptures teach that giving is better than receiving. This is seen by the words and actions of Jesus. In the Gospel of John, Jesus washes his disciples' feet, giving a practical example of humble service. In the Parable of the Sheep and Goats, Jesus taught that those who serve others are praised and those who do not are condemned. The letters in the New Testament also show how important it is for Christians to serve others.

'Do not forget to entertain strangers, for by so
doing some people have entertained angels
without knowing it.'

(Hebrews 13:2)

'So whether you eat or drink or whatever you
do, do it all for the glory of God.'

(1 Corinthians 10:31)

Hinduism

Service of others is love in action. It shows unselfishness and the sense of unity between people. Every selfless act comes from God because it shows no sense of the separate doer.

'Strive constantly to serve the welfare of the
world; by devotion to selfless work one attains
the supreme goal of life.'

(Bhagavad Gita, Chapter 4)

ACTIVITY THREE ••

1. Read the teachings on these pages which show why it is important to serve others in the community. Then copy and complete the following table.

According to …	Service is important because …
Buddhists	
Christians	
Hindus	
Humanists	
Jews	
Muslims	
Sikhs	

2. Look back at the description of the work of Open House (Unit 1, Lesson 4, pages 16—17).

   Matthew is a Christian. How would you say his actions reflect the Christian teachings?

3. Select one of the quotations on these two pages and describe when you have seen it in practice.

Sikhism

Service is very important in Sikhism and is a means of serving, honouring or worshipping. God is not separate from people and so service to humanity is a form of worship. True service (seva) can be through any type of work but must be without gain and in **humility**.

'Cursed are the hands and feet that engage not in seva.'

(Bhai Gurdas 27.10)

'A place in God's court can only be attained if we do service to others in the world.'

(Guru Granth Sahib 26)

Islam

The Qur'an and Hadith teach that Muslims should help everyone. Being a true Muslim means that you must serve others and seek no reward for yourself.

'They feed with food the needy wretch, the orphan, and the prisoners, for love of Him, saying, "We wish for no reward nor thanks from you."'

(Qur'an 76 8—9)

NOW TRY THIS ••••••••••••••••••

'Recall the face of the poorest and most helpless person whom you may have seen and ask yourself if the step you contemplate is going to be of any use to him.'

(Part of the Gandhi Talisman)

Can you identify two different situations where someone might put the teachings of Gandhi into practice?

35

3. What roles do religions play in the community?

SKILLS

- **interpreting** a story
- **using** a range of sources to investigate the role religions can play within a community
- **expressing** an opinion concerning religious involvement in your local community

Below is a traditional Jewish story.

ACTIVITY ONE

1. If you had to write the meaning of the story as a text message what would you write?

2. As a group, choose a title for the story from the suggestions below. Discuss the title you have chosen and be ready to justify your choice to the rest of the class:

a) A Jewish story

b) Everyone has a talent

c) What clowns do

d) Communities work together

e) Working for good will be rewarded

f) Love in action.

Rabbi Barucha of Huza often went to the marketplace at Lapet. One day, the prophet Elijah appeared to him there, and Rabbi Barucha asked him, 'Is there anyone among all these people who will have a share in the world to come?'

Elijah answered, 'There is none.'

Later, two men came to the marketplace, and Elijah said to Rabbi Barucha, 'Those two will have a share in the world to come.'

Rabbi Barucha asked the newcomers, 'What is your occupation?' They replied, 'We are clowns. When we see someone who is sad, we cheer him up. When we see two people quarrelling, we try to make peace between them.'

Faithworks

Many religious communities take a particular interest in the local community in which they are established by seeking to put their faith and values into action.

Faithworks is a Christian organisation which meets regularly with influential decision makers to ensure faith-based projects are a high priority.

One of their campaigns is to support traveller communities who are often discriminated against in Britain. In May 2003, 15-year-old Johnny Delaney was attacked and beaten to death by a gang of youths. Witnesses described how Johnny's attackers repeatedly kicked him when he was lying on the ground. When a passer-by shouted at them to stop they were told, 'He deserves it – he is only a gypsy.'

Faithworks actively encourages faith communities to support traveller communities through a range of different activities such as:

- befriending travellers
- supporting them with planning application forms
- arranging for doctors to visit the sites to help with any medical problems
- educating the local community and pupils at schools about traveller culture and encouraging people to revise any prejudices.

One of the priests involved in Faithworks stressed how important the work was:

> According to the Bible how we treat them is how we treat Christ.

△ *Tony Blair giving his support at a Faithworks meeting.*

ACTIVITY TWO ••••••••••••

1. Some people believe that faith communities should not get involved in local issues while other people believe their actions can support a community. There are more examples on pages 38 and 39 of how people help their communities. Consider the material in this lesson and complete the following statements to give different views.

> Faith communities should not interfere with the local community because ...

> Faith communities should be actively involved in the local community because ...

2. How would you respond to someone who says: 'You have to be religious to care for others'?

37

In the last lesson (pages 32–35) we learnt *why* different religious traditions want to serve the community. Now we will investigate how they do this.

The pictures here and opposite give some examples of the many different ways faith communities serve their local communities.

▶ *A Salvation Army shelter provides Christmas dinner.*

◀ *The Hare Krishna Food for Life programme.*

▶ *A church notice board, showing the different community programmes it offers.*

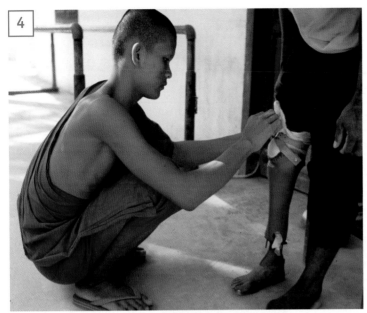

4

▲ A Buddhist monk working in a medical centre in Thailand.

5

▲ Fence building in the UK, maintaining a Gurdwara.

ACTIVITY THREE ....

1. Copy out the table below and use the pictures on these pages to complete it.

Picture	Religion	What is happening?

2. Add a fourth column to your table to explain how the picture relates to the religious teachings of that religion. (You might find it helpful to look at pages 34–35 in the previous lesson.)

3. Look back over lessons 2 and 3 (pages 32–39) and write an acrostic for the word 'service'.

S

E

R

V

I

C

E

NOW TRY THIS ....

Explain this **Sufi** teaching to your partner.

Past the seeker as he prayed came the ill and the beggar and the beaten. And seeing them he cried, 'Great God, how is it that a loving creator can see such things and yet do nothing about them? God said, 'I did do something. I made you.'

4. Why are there different types of schools?

Schools play an important role in most communities. They:

- provide education for pupils
- hold evening classes for adults
- organise many activities where all members of the local community can meet.

Within Britain there are many types of secondary schools. There are a growing number of schools that belong to faith groups or religions.

ACTIVITY ONE

Look at the pictures 1–4 and copy and complete the table. One example has been done for you. (Leave space for a fourth column.)

Picture	Religion	My evidence
3	Jewish	Hebrew on the wall and hanukiah light [see page 60].

There are many similarities between faith and non-faith schools. All schools, for example, aim to provide a good education for all their pupils. However, there are also some differences which reflect the teachings and practices of a particular religious tradition. These are often seen in the school's mission statement as well as in different parts of the school day.

All the food in my school is halal. This is important as I am a Muslim.

Uzma

Our teachers are not of all the same religion.

Bryn

At the start of each lesson we say the Lord's Prayer.

Shirin

When it is a special day, like Rosh Hashanah, the school is closed so we can celebrate with our families.

Anna

We go on many retreats with our school where we learn more about our religion.

Sophie

In RE we learn most about Hinduism although we do learn about other religions as well.

Henna

I wear my hijab in all the lessons in school – most of the Muslim girls do.

Nasima

We do a lot of fund-raising for charities in the school.

Fran

We are taught in school how important it is to care for other human beings.

Salli

ACTIVITY TWO ················

1. Draw a fourth column on your table from Activity One. Using the quotes on this page write the name of the pupils you think might attend that school.

2. Think about the practices in your own school and identify the quotes that are the same as your school and those that are different.

64 per cent of people oppose faith schools

Government set to increase the number of faith schools

Many people have different views about whether or not there should be faith schools.

Although a recent poll showed that 64 per cent of people oppose faith schools, many parents want their children to attend them and the government has decided to allow more to be built.

ACTIVITY THREE

1. Read through this list of statements (i–xv) and with a partner divide them into three categories:

   a) against faith schools

   b) for faith schools

   c) no evidence for or against.

   i) More people stay at school until they are 18.

   ii) I am really glad I go to a school where there are pupils from lots of religions and none.

   iii) Going to a school where all the pupils belong to my religion has given me pride in my identity. In my other school some pupils laughed at my religion.

   iv) Religious Education is a compulsory subject at school up to the age of 18.

   v) Schools in England were originally set up by the Christian Churches.

   vi) One-third of schools are faith-based schools.

   vii) Faith schools allow pupils to worship together.

   viii) Faith schools have shared aims.

   ix) Pupils cannot learn about other people's religions if they are **segregated**.

   x) Pupils may not have the same beliefs as their parents.

   xi) Teachers would understand more about the pupils' backgrounds in a faith school.

   xii) Society is multi-cultural and schools should be as well.

   xiii) If schools are not **integrated** then it means the local community is not integrated.

   xiv) Friends may be separated after junior school.

   xv) People have the right to be educated in the tradition of their own beliefs and values.

2. With a partner select the three arguments which you think are most convincing either for faith schools or against faith schools. Then find a pair of pupils who have chosen different arguments and try to convince them you are right.

NOW TRY THIS

Many people are concerned that if pupils from different faith backgrounds do not meet together in schools they will not learn to co-operate with each other or know about each other's beliefs and traditions.

Imagine you have to organise a weekend at a **retreat** centre where pupils from different faith schools will be attending. What events would you organise and why?

5. Why do some religious communities live apart?

SKILLS

- **considering** why some religious communities live separately from the local community
- **sorting and categorising** information from a range of sources
- **thinking about** the challenges of belonging to religious communities

Many religious traditions have communities which live separately from the local community. These are called closed communities. Faith members go there to devote themselves totally to their faith, undisturbed by worldly life.

For example, in Christianity monks or nuns living in **monasteries** or **convents** believe that leaving the worldly life helps them to be **contemplative** and not distracted by worldly matters. They live under an arrangement called **the Rule** which is the guidance of that particular community and often means they take three distinct **vows**.

1. Vow of **poverty** – to give up ownership of all worldly possessions to show complete trust in God and to understand what it is like to be poor.

2. Vow of **chastity** – to give up family life in order to follow Jesus. Monks and nuns give up sexual relations and do not have a husband or wife.

3. Vow of **obedience** – to be obedient to the Rule.

▲ *The three knots on these Franciscan monks' cords symbolise the three vows. What other ways do people show the vows or promises they have made?*

◀ *Along with tending to and picking vegetables in the convent garden, what other activities might nuns be involved in?*

ACTIVITY ONE ....

1. Write down each vow and consider the implications of each. One example has been done for you.

POVERTY	CHASTITY	OBEDIENCE
having no savings	never being a parent	doing things I don't want to do

2. Compare your findings with a partner and discuss which one of the three vows you think would be most difficult to keep.

3. Do you think it is a good idea that people live in monasteries and convents?

   Below are some possible answers to this question. With a partner sort them into answers saying that it is a good thing and answers saying that it is not. Try to decide which side of the debate you would be on.

   a) The only way that people can really devote themselves to God is by living with other people like them.

   b) By living in a closed community they do not really know what is happening in the real world.

   c) By not having a family they can devote themselves to God.

   d) It does not mean they are shut off from the world; many take a wider role to help the community.

   e) It is not natural to live apart from different types of people.

The Amish

The Amish is a religious group who consider that it is important for all members of the faith to live as a community. There are about 130,000 followers who live mainly in America. They try to keep themselves separate from the local community as they have different beliefs and practices. They do not seek to convert people and always try to keep marriage within the community.

Men follow the Hebrew scriptures and so wear beards when they are married.

We do not wear moustaches because they are connected with the military and we do not believe in any war at all.

We are **conscientious objectors** and never resort to violence.

We are forbidden to swear oaths in court.

At a wedding the bride will wear either blue or purple.

Like many Muslims and some Orthodox Jews we do not usually allow photographs of our full faces as we believe that goes against the Ten Commandments: 'You shall not make a graven image …'.

Women wear a long dress with long sleeves and usually wear a bonnet.

Very few Amish have cars; we use horse and buggy for transport.

We do not have phones or TVs or computers although we can get them in an emergency.

We believe in living our life quite separate from the rest of the world partly because of the persecution we have suffered and partly so that we do not become 'polluted'.

We are not miserable; we have lots of celebrations. We celebrate all the traditional Christian holy days.

Men work on the farm and women work in the home.

Children normally stop going to school at 14 and start helping on the farm or in the home.

We do not draw electricity, as this would connect us to the world.

We do not normally build churches to worship in but worship in the homes of members. It is the people not the building which is really the church.

We do not collect money such as pensions from the state.

ACTIVITY THREE ....

1. What do you think the Amish mean by not wanting to be polluted?

2. With a partner make a list of what the Amish might consider as 'pollution' in the rest of the world.

NOW TRY THIS ....

Many people now travel to America to see how the Amish live.

1. Why do you think they would want to do this?

2. Should the tourist industry promote visits to see the lifestyle of the Amish?

SUMMARY OF UNIT 2

Lesson 2

You have learned about different religious and non-religious views on service.

Lesson 3

You have learned about how different religions serve the community.

Lesson 1

You have learned about the importance of religious communities.

What is the impact of different religions on the community?

Lesson 4

You have learned about some of the differences between faith and non-faith schools.

Lesson 5

You have learned why some religious communities choose to live apart from other communities.

UNIT 3: WHAT INSIGHTS DO DIFFERENT RELIGIONS BRING TO GOOD AND EVIL?

Lesson 1: How can people tell the difference between good and evil?

◎ Think about how people know the difference between good and evil.

◎ Investigate what is meant by 'conscience'.

◎ Read about conscientious objectors.

Lesson 2: Why is there evil?

◎ Think about the difference between natural and moral evil.

◎ Learn about Christian, Hindu and Humanist ideas regarding evil.

◎ Form your own opinion on the nature of evil.

Lesson 3: How is light used as a symbol?

◎ Investigate how light is used as a symbol.

◎ Discover how different religions use light in their practices and worship.

◎ Express your own understanding of light as a symbol.

Lesson 4: How do we learn from our role models?

◎ Consider the different features of role models.

◎ Learn about the importance of Krishna for many Hindus.

◎ Form your own opinions on people who inspire and influence you.

Lesson 5: What attitudes do people have to heaven?

◎ Consider how heaven has been expressed through words and pictures.

◎ Compare different religious attitudes to the existence of heaven.

◎ Evaluate and form your own opinion on the concept of heaven.

What insights do different religions bring to good and evil?

1. How can people tell the difference between good and evil?

SKILLS

- **thinking about** the difference between good and evil
- **expressing** ideas about the role of conscience
- **finding out** about conscientious objectors

One of the main differences between human beings and animals is the ability to make moral decisions to do good or evil. Living and acting according to what you think is right is called acting **morally** but acting according to what you know is wrong is called acting **immorally**.

ACTIVITY ONE •••••••••••••••

The two images below were used for a campaign by the human rights protest group Amnesty International, along with the words, 'We're an extraordinary species, we humans. We can send one man to the moon. And millions more to the hell of the killing fields.'

1. In pairs discuss what you think the poster's message is.

2. Imagine you are from the campaigns department of Amnesty International. Decide how you would lay out the images for a poster and what title you would give it. You will need to have your reason ready to persuade the department.

3. Write down or make a collage of two pairs of examples that would show the difference between good and evil.

◀ *These photos show Buzz Aldrin walking on the moon, and some of the victims of the genocide in Cambodia.*

The study of what makes something right or wrong is called **ethics**.

But how do people know if they are doing good or evil?

Are they born with that knowledge?

Are they taught it?

Many people claim that they know when they have done something right or wrong because of something within them called a **conscience**. It is hard to explain what a conscience is as pictures cannot be taken of it and it cannot be seen. There are many different views concerning the nature of a conscience, although most people refer to it as a feeling within you.

1

The Oxford Dictionary describes conscience as 'a moral sense of right and wrong, especially as felt by a person and affecting behaviour'.

2

St Jerome spoke about people's power of distinguishing good from evil as 'the spark of conscience ... by which we discern that we sin'.

3

Sigmund Freud was a famous psychiatrist who described conscience as our sense of moral right and wrong which enforces the rules of behaviour we were taught when we were young.

4

Joseph Butler was an Anglican priest who described conscience as 'the voice within us'. He said it is a natural guide given by God which should therefore always be obeyed.

5

The American journalist H.L. Mencken described conscience as 'the inner voice that warns us that someone might be looking'.

ACTIVITY TWO ....

1. Below is a list (a–g) of the descriptions connected with the conscience.

   Read the speech bubbles 1–5 again and select one description for each:

   a) *inner or internal*

   b) *an outside force*

   c) **the voice of God**

   d) *developed by our parents*

   e) **helps us judge right from wrong**

   f) *tells us the sort of behaviour we should follow*

   g) **invisible**.

2. If *you* had to select a description of conscience which would you choose from the list above?

   Be ready to justify your decision to your partner.

3. You have been asked to produce an illustration for Year 7 students to explain what you think conscience is. In your drawing or design you need to consider many questions such as:

   • What colours would you use?

   • Would the conscience be on its own or would there be something else in your illustration?

   • What shape is it?

Many people agree that conscience is a driving force for doing good and is a major factor in giving them the motivation to stand up for what they believe in. They often show this by taking part in demonstrations or protest marches.

Civil rights campaigners such as Martin Luther King and Gandhi showed the important role that conscience played in their decisions.

'Expediency asks the question – is it politic?

Vanity asks the question – is it popular?

But conscience asks the question – is it right?

And there comes a time when one must take a position that is neither safe, nor politic, nor popular, but one must take it because it is right.'

(Martin Luther King)

▶ *Martin Luther King*

'The only tyrant I accept in this world is still the voice within.'

(Gandhi)

▶ *Gandhi was a politician who led non-violent protest movements. What examples of non-violent protest can you think of?*

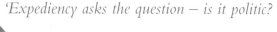

ACTIVITY THREE ●●●●●●●●●●●

1. Read the quote from Martin Luther King again. Discuss with a partner a time when you have had to make a decision that was not popular but you knew was right. Try to identify what influenced your decision.

2. In Martin Luther King's book *Strength to Love* he wrote:

   'I submit that an individual who breaks a law that conscience tells him is unjust, and who willingly accepts the penalty of imprisonment in order to arouse the conscience of the community over its injustice, is in reality expressing the highest respect for the law.'

   What issues might someone's conscience be opposed to? Try to find an example for each of the following categories:

   • Equal rights

   • Animal rights

   • Sanctity of life.

Throughout history some people have refused to fight for their country. They are called **conscientious objectors** because they refuse to fight for a state. They disapprove of the **conflict** for religious, political or ethical reasons. Many members of the Society of Friends (**Quakers**) believe there is a part of God in everyone and that more can be achieved by appealing to the love and goodness in people.

▶ *These Quakers are showing their disapproval of war and violence. What do you think the image on their banner symbolises?*

Most Quakers follow the Peace Testimony, written in 1660. This is a short extract:

'We utterly deny all outward wars and strife and fightings with outward weapons, for any end, or under any pretence whatever. And this is our testimony to the world … that the spirit of Christ, which leads us all into all Truth, will never move us to fight any war against any man with outward weapons, neither for the kingdom of Christ, nor for the kingdoms of the world.'

NOW TRY THIS ....

Rewrite the Peace Testimony in your own words.

Do you think a teaching that was written over 350 years ago is relevant today?

2. Why is there evil?

▲ *Global misuse of the environment creates an increase in famine.*

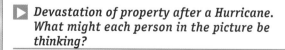

▷ *Devastation of property after a Hurricane. What might each person in the picture be thinking?*

▲ *Deforestation, or the stripping of trees from an area, can lead to soil erosion and famine.*

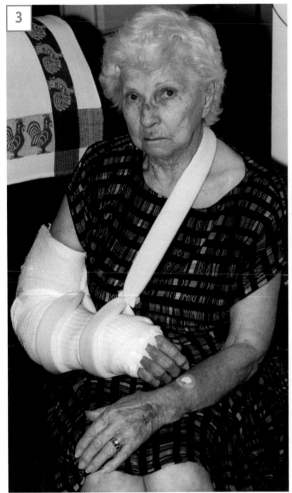

▲ *Injuries as a result of a mugging in the street.*

▶ *Why do people bully others?*

We often hear of 'evil acts' but what is actually meant by the term?

There are two types of evil:

1. Natural evil – this refers to events that cause suffering but have nothing to do with human actions, for example earthquakes.

2. Moral evil – this refers to human actions which cause suffering to others, for example torture.

ACTIVITY ONE ....

1. Look at the pictures above and opposite. Do they show natural or moral evil or neither?

2. Give one reason why you think each situation happened.

3. What do you think is the difference between a 'bad action' and an 'evil action'?

All religions have a teaching about the nature of evil although individual members may have different beliefs. For all religious believers one question that must be considered is 'if God is good how can evil exist?'

Look at the views of Jill, Darshan and Sunita.

Jill is 14 and is a member of the Anglican Church.

'Whenever something evil happens I think how could a good God, a God who is everywhere, let it happen? I might read a passage in the Bible, like the story of Job, or go to my minister but I know in the end I have to decide for myself.

I believe God is all loving but he has given people free will to do evil or to do good. It is our conscience that guides us.

We are not puppets. It is up to us and we will get our rewards (or not) when we die. I do believe in an evil force and I believe that that force can tempt us to do bad things. I know not all my Christian friends believe this. This world isn't meant to be paradise or perfect. That's still to come.

I suppose at the end I believe that we can't understand God's reason – maybe sometimes some good can come out of tragedies by the way that people work together but we just don't know. We can't see the whole picture.'

Darshan is 13 and a Hindu.

'In Hinduism it is ignorance not an external force like the devil which is the root of evil. Only self-conscious beings can be evil as they choose to do harm to others or to themselves. By choosing to harm others you are harming yourself and so you must be ignorant to do that. Christians use the term evil but in Sanskrit it is 'avidya' which actually means 'lack of knowledge'.

You could say God is the ultimate source of evil as God gave us free choice to do good acts or evil acts. Hindus know that, through **karma**, if we do evil acts we will eventually be punished. Evil and good are all a part of life. That's why the god Kali is associated with good as well as evil.

We learn from a very early age that evil is a part of the **Samsara** and that whatever evil people do in this life they will be paid back for it in another life. We don't have a force like Satan in Hinduism nor do we believe in Hell.'

Sunita is 13 and a humanist.

'Some humanists avoid using the word evil, but when we do it usually means something so dreadful that the words 'wicked' or 'awful' aren't strong enough. We don't believe in an outside force like the devil, nor is it seen as a test of our faith. Humanists do not believe in an afterlife so there is no idea of people being punished for evil acts after death. We believe that evil events such as floods and other disasters happen by natural causes or just by chance.

Humans have freedom of choice to do good or bad but really there are so few acts that can be called evil compared to all the good acts that people do.'

NOW TRY THIS ....

Choose two of the views on page 56 then copy and complete the Venn diagram.

In the outside circles write the differences in the beliefs about evil and in the middle list any similarities.

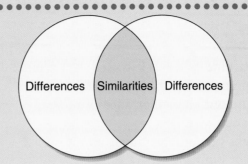

Differences | Similarities | Differences

ACTIVITY TWO ....

There are many different views and beliefs about evil. Some are given in the quotes below. Pick the three you most agree with and the one you least agree with.

Why have you picked these? Discuss your choice with a partner.

Albert Einstein (a scientist)

The world is a dangerous place to live, not because of the people who are evil, but because of the people who don't do anything about it.

Martin Luther King (a Christian minister and Human Rights leader)

Whoever accepts evil without protesting against it is really co-operating with it.

Swami Vivekananda (a Hindu religious leader)

We have no theory of evil. We call it ignorance.

The Bible *Job 18:21*

Evil comes to those who do evil ... people get what they deserve.

The Bible *1 Timothy 6:10*

Love of money is the root of all evil.

Epicurus (a Greek philosopher)

If God exists, is good, loving and all powerful why does he let evil happen?

Edmund Burke (a Christian philosopher)

It is necessary only for the good to do nothing for evil to happen.

3. How is light used as a symbol?

SKILLS

- **identifying** how light is used as a symbol in religious teachings and ritual
- **finding out** the importance of light in many religions
- **expressing** your own ideas about the symbol of light

Light is used in many cultures and religions as a sign of bringing hope and light in the darkness.

▼ *Visitors and locals remember victims of the 2003 tsunami in Patong, Thailand.*

▲ *Diva lamps are lit at the festival of Divali. They welcome Lakshmi, the goddess of fortune, and are a reminder of the lights used to guide Rama and Sita out of the forest.*

◄ *Christians prepare for Christmas through the season of Advent. The advent candle is lit to count down the days of Advent and to symbolise Jesus as the 'light of the world' (*John 1.18*).*

4

▲ *Candles are often used to symbolise someone's birthday.*

5

▲ *Two candles are often placed on an altar to represent Jesus as human and divine. They are often lit before prayer and worship.*

6

◄ *Lighthouses help to guide ships.*

7

▲ *Paper lanterns are lit on Nagasaki Day in Japan to remind people of the dropping of the atomic bomb on the city in 1945. Over 22 per cent of buildings in the city were destroyed by fire and there were between 50,000–100,000 casualties.*

ACTIVITY ONE ••••••••••••••

1. Look at pictures 1–7 on these pages and for each picture choose a reason from the list below to say why you think the light has been used. You may decide that there is more than one reason for some of the pictures.

   a) To welcome.

   b) To celebrate a happy time.

   c) An act of prayer and devotion.

   d) As a source of guidance.

   e) To represent the dual nature of Christ.

   f) As a mark of remembrance and hope.

   g) As a mark of time for preparation.

2. Can you identify any other occasions when light is used as a symbol?

There are many different ways and reasons why light is used but for everyone it shares a common purpose of leading to or guiding into something positive. Light is used as a symbol in the teachings and rituals of many religious traditions.

Hinduism

The Bhagavad Gita talks of 'light of wisdom'. Once the light of wisdom touches the heart then one begins to see and understand everything. Often

before and during worship diva lamps are lit to symbolise the divine light and presence of God.

Buddhism

Candles are often placed on Buddhist shrines. In some monasteries butter lamps are lit as offerings of light dedicated to world peace.

Jainism

The lighting of a lamp is one of the most important rituals in the Jain way of life. Ghee lamps are lit at home, in temples and for the festival of Diwali to symbolise the right knowledge that helps Jains to have right faith and right conduct. Many Jains light the lamp as their first act of the day. For Jains the light is a symbol of divine knowledge that removes the darkness which causes negative feelings, fear and ignorance.

Islam

In Islam, Allah is described as follows:

'Allah is the Light of the Heavens and the earth.'

(Sura 24.35, Qur'an)

By using the word 'light' it shows the illumination that Allah brings to all those willing to be guided.

Judaism

There are many references to light in Judaism. Shabbat, the day of rest and peace, begins with the lighting of two candles. For each of the eight days of **Hanukkah** a candle is lit as a reminder of the miracle when there was only enough oil for one day, yet it lasted for eight until more was found. Hanukkah is a winter festival so the candles in the dark are a sign of hope.

The **Ner Tamid** light can be found in synagogues. This is an everlasting light which symbolises God's presence.

Christianity

For Christians the symbol of light is very important. Candles are often used in some churches because they represent the presence of God, guidng people into truth. Jesus is also referred to as the 'Light' in the Gospel of John:

'That was the true Light which lighteth every man that cometh into the world.'

Sikhism

Guru actually means the destroyer of darkness and so the giver of light. The darkness is the darkness of ignorance which can be removed only by gaining spiritual knowledge from the Guru.

In November Sikhs celebrate two festivals, both of which are connected with the theme of light. Diwali celebrates the release of Guru Hargobind from prison and he was welcomed with a row of diva lamps. The second event is the birth of Guru Nanak, the founder of the Sikh faith. This is described as sunrise leading to complete light:

'The true Guru, Nanak, was revealed
The fog lifted and the light descended on the world
It was like the sun rising
The stars disappeared and the darkness vanished.'

(Written by Bhai Gurdas in the seventeenth century)

ACTIVITY TWO

Read about the different beliefs and practices and copy and complete the following table. The first entry has been done for you.

Religion	How is light used in worship or ritual	Why?
Buddhism	Lamps are lit	For world peace

ACTIVITY THREE

1. Produce a spider diagram to show how light is used to symbolise different concepts. Some examples of different concepts are given below:

   a) celebration   d) guidance

   b) freedom   e) truth

   c) knowledge of ignorance   f) divine presence.

   In your diagram give examples.

2. A famous saying by Carl Sagan is:

   'Why curse the darkness
   When you have the power to light
   At least one candle?'

   In your own words write out what you think is the meaning of this quote.

NOW TRY THIS

The civil rights leader Martin Luther King said:

'Darkness cannot drive out darkness; only light can do that. Hate cannot drive out hate; only love can do that.'

Either write a story or design a picture to illustrate this quotation.

KEY WORDS

Guru   in Sikhism it is used to refer to one of the ten historic leaders of the community and also of God

Hanukkah/Chanukah   Jewish festival of lights

Ner Tamid   eternal light found in synagogues

4. How do we learn from our role models?

SKILLS

- **identifying** the different features of role models
- **interpreting** a range of sources to understand the significance of Krishna for many Hindus
- **reflecting upon** the people who inspire and influence you

2. A guide for my life is the **Hadith** or sayings of the Prophet Muhammad. Whenever I am unsure about how to act I always feel guidance from the teachings. They are timeless. Although they were from over 1400 years ago they are still relevant to today.

1. Whenever I am stuck in a situation I think to myself what would Jesus do? It's the actions of Jesus that inspire me – particularly the way he mixed with people who other people would have nothing to do with.

▲ *The Hadith are the words, actions and instructions of the Prophet Muhammad. If there is no clear answer in the Qur'an then many Muslims will seek advice from the Hadith.*

3. It's Bob Geldof's attitude which inspires me. People often criticise him but he just gets on and does it. He really does make a difference.

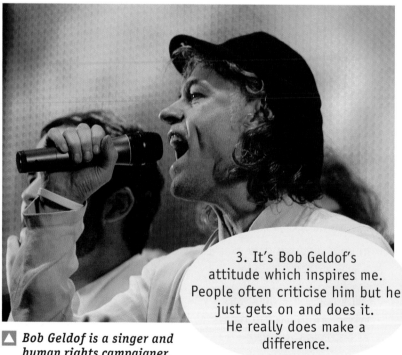

▲ *Bob Geldof is a singer and human rights campaigner. He has organised many concerts to put pressure on political leaders to solve the problem of poverty in Africa.*

▲ *What qualities of Jesus do you think the artist Hunt shows in his painting?*

▲ *Ellen MacArthur sailed around the world non-stop on her own. It took over 71 days and 14 hours.*

ACTIVITY ONE ·················

1. Read again all the descriptions of the role models and select which characteristics below are identified in each:

   a) good looks

   b) skill and determination

   c) wise teachings

   d) lots of money

   e) inspirational actions

   f) courage

   g) positive attitude

   h) dedication

   i) commitment.

2. Which four characteristics listed above do you think are most important for a role model?

3. Compare your answers with a partner and choose one person who you think has these characteristics. Be ready to justify your selection to the rest of the class.

4. I feel so inspired when I read about the courage of Ellen MacArthur. She really pushes herself to achieve her goals.

5. My **role model** is Tiger Woods. I am always inspired by the skill, determination and hard work he puts into playing golf.

▶ *Tiger Woods was the first golfer to win all four majors.*

63

Many people learn the difference between good and evil through the examples of teachings and actions of key individuals within a religious tradition. For Christians this might be Jesus and for Muslims the Prophet Muhammad.

In Hinduism there are many **deities** who may be special to individuals but one who is very popular is **Krishna**.

He was born in a jail in the state of Mathura which was ruled by his wicked uncle who had taken the throne from his parents. Krishna was miraculously rescued and taken to live in **Vrindavan** where he was brought up by his foster parents. During his life many events occurred which showed Krishna's important qualities. The legends of the life of Krishna appear in the Bhagavad Purana and his teachings are found in the Bhagavad Gita.

Event 2

Krishna overcame a many-headed serpent called **Kaliya** who had been causing the village to suffer by polluting it with poison. Krishna battled with the serpent and made the serpent ask for forgiveness. The image of Krishna dancing on the serpent's head shows his powers to overcome evil.

▶ *Murtis like this can be found in many Hindu temples.*

Event 1

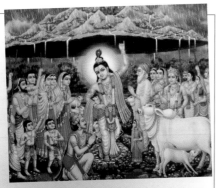

▲ *Krishna saves Mount Goverdhan. Why do you think there are cows in the picture?*

Indra, the feared God of the Sky, sent great storms to punish people because they were charmed by Krishna and seemed to forget about him. The shivering cattle and terrified people turned to Krishna to save them. The waters were rising dangerously so Krishna protected his people by picking up Mount Goverdhan on his little finger and lifting it high above the flood waters. He gathered all the living creatures to save them from the floods. When Lord Indra saw this he accepted the powers of Krishna.

Event 3

The Bhagavad Gita tells how **Arjuna** has to go into battle with his cousins and teachers. He cannot bear the idea that he will have to try to injure them. Krishna advises him that sometimes it is necessary to fight to overcome evil forces. Krishna tells Arjuna that:

▲ *Krishna is standing to give Arjuna advice. What clues in the picture tell you that it is Krishna?*

* as a prince and soldier he has to fight for the good of his people

* he can only cause death of people's bodies as he cannot hurt their souls

* he is not fighting for personal gain but for the benefit of people.

Krishna teaches about the value of karma and of doing one's duty with detachment, without thought of reward.

ACTIVITY TWO ···············

1. Draw the outline of Krishna below. Using the three events opposite, write around the outline what you have learned so far about the *external features* of Krishna, for example events in his life, what he did, what he looks like. Then inside the outline in another colour write what *qualities* he showed. Some examples have been done for you.

Brave

Born in a prison

2. How would you reply to the following?

'It doesn't matter whether Krishna lived or not. His actions are an inspiration.'

ACTIVITY THREE ············

1. Do you have role models?

2. List the ways that you show respect for them.

NOW TRY THIS ···········

In the Bhagavad Gita Krishna asks:

'Surrender then thy actions unto me, live in me, concentrate thine intellect on me and think always of me.'

How do you think Hindus might do this?

KEY WORDS

Deities gods

Hadith stories about or sayings of the Prophet Muhammad

Janmashtami the festival celebrating Krishna's birth

Krishna one of the most popular of the Hindu gods who came to earth in human form

Hindus show their respect for Krishna each year by celebrating his birthday on the festival of **Janmashtami**. He is believed to have been born at midnight so during the festival many Hindus stay up past this time. Often a cot is placed on the shrine in the temple to represent his birth and the story of how Krishna was rescued from the prison is told. The ceremony is often televised so that Hindus throughout the world can watch the event.

▲ *At Janmashtami children are often dressed like Krishna.*

5. What attitudes do people have to heaven?

We may often hear these sayings or say the word '**heaven**' but what do we really mean?

For thousands of years people have tried to find out if heaven exists and have imagined what it may be like.

> It's like being in heaven.

> It's heavenly.

> Heaven only knows.

ACTIVITY ONE

1. Work in pairs. One of you should have a copy of the book.

   Sit with your back to your partner and if you have the book describe six main features in the picture to the right by Gustave Dore. Your partner should draw a picture from your description. Remember the use of certain colours may be important.

2. Look at the picture with your partner and answer the following questions.

   a) Why do you think the artist has used these colours?

   b) Why do you think it is hard to see the features of the two people?

   c) What is the feeling expressed by the picture?

▶ *Is this your view of heaven?*

Heaven is a real place located in the highest part of the universe.

Heaven doesn't exist – it's just made up.

I always think of heaven as a beautiful garden where there is peace.

The spirits of animals and humans go there after death.

I don't think there is such a place as heaven but I do believe people can produce a heavenly world by being kind to each other.

I don't know what it looks like – but I do know God is there.

I don't know and I don't care what happens after you are dead.

Just as **hell** is being separate from God so heaven is being in God's presence.

I don't know – I think it's far more important that we try to create a heavenly place on earth while we are alive.

ACTIVITY TWO ....

1. A survey asked 500 people to give their views on heaven. Above are some of the replies. With a partner read each of them and decide which argue:

   a) there is no heaven

   b) heaven is a real place

   c) heaven is a state of mind, for example, feelings of peace.

2. Now select one view that you agree with and try to illustrate it. Explain why you have used any particular colours or symbols.

Hinduism

Hindus believe in **reincarnation** – that when you die your soul is born again in a different body. This happens time after time until you break out of the cycle. Breaking free is called **moksha** and can only happen when wisdom replaces ignorance. For some Hindus moksha is like reaching heaven.

◀ *This painting,* **Changing Bodies,** *depicts the idea that, just as the soul continuously passes in this body, from boyhood to youth to old age, the soul similarly passes into another body at death. What would you draw to describe reincarnation?*

Christianity

Christians believe heaven is where God is. When they die, they hope their soul will go to heaven to begin a new life with God. Heaven is sometimes pictured as an actual place where God has his kingdom. In the book of Revelation, St John paints this picture of heaven:

'I looked and saw a door to Heaven, and a voice like a trumpet, said to me, "Come." There I saw God sitting on an emerald throne, surrounded by a rainbow.'

Baha'i

Followers of Baha'i believe that heaven is the next world where your spirit or soul lives. It is described as a garden of happiness or a heavenly river but it is really where God is. **Baha'u'llah**'s son told people to think of God as a kind gardener who takes a shrub from a dry rocky place and plants it in rich soil where it can flourish and grow. The shrub is like your soul.

Humanism

Humanists do not believe in a heaven or any form of life after death. They believe that the only ways people can live on are through the work they have done, the relationships they have had and other people's memories of them.

Islam

For Muslims, heaven or paradise is a place where people who have followed Allah on earth will live forever, close to Allah in perfect peace and **harmony**. Not everyone goes to heaven. On the **Day of Judgement**, Allah will judge them according to how well or wickedly they have lived. The Qur'an states that the true nature of paradise lies beyond human understanding. The term paradise comes from paradisa, the Persian word for garden. In the Qur'an paradise is described as a beautiful garden.

'On that day there will be joyful faces of people in the garden of delights. A gushing fountain shall be there and soft couches with goblets placed before them, silk cushions and rich carpets.'

(Surah 37:47, Qur'an)

ACTIVITY THREE ● ● ● ● ● ● ● ● ● ● ● ●

Read the different teachings again and decide which teachings would agree with the following statements.

a) Heaven is where God is.

b) Your spirit moves on into heaven.

c) Heaven is often described as a beautiful garden.

d) There is no heaven.

NOW TRY THIS ● ● ● ● ● ● ● ● ● ● ●

Imagine a person is coming into your class who has found out the answers to what heaven is. They have only five minutes to explain what they have found out.

You are able to ask only three questions.

What would you ask?

KEY WORDS

Baha'u'llah   founder of the Baha'is (1817–1892)

Day of Judgement   when God makes his final decision on how a person has acted during their life

Harmony   in agreement

Heaven   where God is found to his full extent

Hell   where God is absent

Moksha   release or liberation. Usually used to refer to becoming free from the cycle of birth and death

Reincarnation   a belief that human beings are born into new lives in this world after they die

SUMMARY OF UNIT 3

Lesson 2

You have learned that there are different views about why evil exists.

Lesson 3

You have learned how light is used as a symbol for goodness and hope.

What insights do different religions bring to good and evil?

Lesson 1

You have learned about how people distinguish between good and evil.

Lesson 4

You have learned about role models and how Krishna is considered as a role model for many Hindus.

Lesson 5

You have learned that there are different views about the existence and nature of heaven.

UNIT 4: WHAT DO RELIGIONS SAY ABOUT THE USE OF MONEY AND OTHER RESOURCES?

Lesson 1: What is the religious attitude to wealth?

◎ Investigate the teachings of different religions about the importance of wealth.

◎ Consider and evaluate two religious attitudes about the importance of wealth.

◎ Think about the transitory nature of wealth.

Lesson 2: What do religions say about ways of gaining wealth?

◎ Think about the impact of the Five Precepts for Buddhist daily life.

◎ Consider the role of ethics in businesses.

◎ Learn about attitudes to gambling from two religions.

Lesson 3: What about the earth's resources?

◎ Think about how humans are damaging the earth.

◎ Form your own opinion concerning how we should care for the earth.

◎ Produce a lesson or presentation on how to treat the earth.

Lesson 4: What do religions say about care for the environment?

◎ Learn about the Christian and Muslim attitude to the environment.

◎ Compare different religious attitudes to stewardship and present information.

Lesson 5: What attitudes do religions have to animals?

◎ Consider how religious beliefs can inspire care for animals.

◎ Compare Buddhist, Hindu and Muslim projects to care for animals.

◎ Read the evidence and form your own opinion on whether Jesus was a vegetarian.

Lesson 6: What makes us strong?

◎ Think about which spiritual qualities you consider are most important.

◎ Investigate a range of sources to discover how people can develop well-being.

◎ Read about the life of Nkosi Johnson and identify his spiritual qualities.

What do religions say about the use of money and other resources?

1. What is the religious attitude to wealth?

SKILLS

- **thinking about** the importance of wealth
  - **identifying** key beliefs about wealth from religious texts
- **interpreting** a range of sources concerning wealth and materialism

Footballers – worth their weight in gold?

House prices on the up again

Designer wardrobe sent me into debt

KEY WORD

Materialistic   concerned with the importance of money

Britain is often described as being a **materialistic** society where people consider wealth and possessions as the most important things in life.

ACTIVITY ONE

1. Look at the newspaper headlines above. Explain what values you think they show.

2. All religions have teachings that show the importance of wealth and how it should be used. Read through the teachings from religious scriptures below and opposite. Which religions would agree with each of the views below?

   a) Money can't make you happy.

   b) Wealth is an illusion that doesn't last.

   c) It's not how much money you've got that's important. It's the good you do with it.

3. Write another view that at least two religions would agree on.

4. Choose one of the religions and read their teachings again. Give two examples of how believers could reflect these teachings in their daily lives.

Buddhism

'Of all gains, good health is the greatest,
Of all wealth, contentment is the greatest.'

(Dhammapada 203:5)

'Whoever in your kingdom is poor, to him let some help be given.'

(Cakkatti Sidhananda Sutta)

Christianity

'Watch out! Be on your guard against all kinds of greed; a man's life does not consist in the abundance of his possessions.'

(Luke 12:15)

'"Good teacher," he asked, "what must I do to inherit eternal life?" ... and Jesus said, "Go, sell everything you have and give to the poor, and you will have treasure in heaven."'

(Mark 10 17:21)

'You cannot serve both God and money.'

(Matthew 6:24)

'The love of money is a root of all kinds of evil.'

(1 Timothy 6:10)

Islam

'A man who helps and spends his time and money looking after widows and the poor holds the same position in the eyes of God as one who fights in a war, or fasts every day and prays the whole night for a number of years.'

(Hadith)

'Richness does not lie in abundance of worldly goods, but true richness is the richness of the soul.'

(Hadith)

Judaism

'Cast but a glance at riches, and they are gone, for they will surely sprout wings and fly off to the sky like an eagle.'

(Proverbs 23:5)

'Who is rich? He who is satisfied with what he has.'

(Ethics of the Fathers)

Hinduism

'The riches of those who are generous never waste away, while those who will not give find none to comfort them.'

(Rig Veda 10:117)

'The desire for wealth can never bring happiness.'

(Mahabharata Shanti Parva)

Sikhism

'Wealth, youth and flowers are short-lived as guests for four short days. Be grateful to God whose bounties you enjoy. Be compassionate to the needy and the people you employ.'

(Guru Granth Sahib 23)

Although many people have tried to take their wealth and possessions with them to another life, none has been successful. It doesn't matter how much wealth we have during our lifetime, it is transitory and therefore will not last.

The storyteller Anthony De Mello in *The Song of the Bird* tells how a wealthy businessman was horrified when he saw a contented fisherman lying beside his boat looking up to the sky.

ACTIVITY TWO

1. In pairs decide what you think the fisherman replied at the end of the story.
2. Decide on a title which expresses the moral of the story.
3. Discuss with a partner times that you have seen or read when wealth has made people unhappy.

NOW TRY THIS ....

Martin Luther King said:

We are prone to judge success by the amount of our salaries or the size of our cars, rather than by the quality of our service and relationship to humanity.

Each year the *Sunday Times* newspaper publishes a list of the most wealthy people in Britain. Imagine a newspaper has asked you to reflect on the Martin Luther King quotation. You are asked to select five people (living or dead) who have given most service and have a high quality relationship to humanity. Who would you choose and how would you justify each choice?

RICH LIST

2. What do religions say about ways of gaining wealth?

SKILLS

- **considering** the impact of the Five Precepts for Buddhists
- **recognising** the role of ethics in businesses
- **understanding** why some religions don't approve of gambling

> As a Buddhist, gaining wealth is a proper goal but this has to be earned honestly. The Noble Eightfold Path teaches us to earn a living in line with Buddhist teachings or right livelihood and the Five Precepts teaches us the moral code we should live by.

Buddhism

The Five Precepts are a Buddhist moral code that is regularly chanted. They are considered to be the ideals for life. They are:

1. not to harm living things
2. not to take what is not given
3. no sexual misconduct
4. no lying
5. not to take drugs or drink to confuse the mind.

ACTIVITY ONE

1. Read the Five Precepts again and select which of these jobs you think might not be approved of by Buddhists:
   a) working in an off-licence
   b) car mechanic
   c) nurse
   d) tobacconist
   e) weapons manufacturer
   f) butcher.

2. Do you think it matters how you gain your money? Discuss the question in groups and be ready to share your ideas with the rest of the class.

Ethics in business

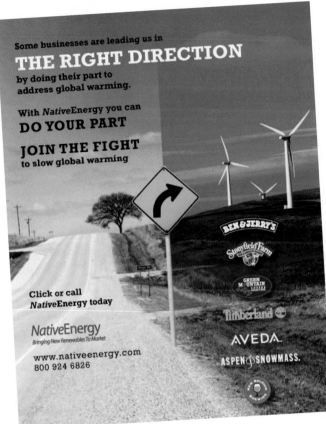

▲ *What do you think these businesses all agree on?*

1. How would you reply to someone who says, 'Businesses should be concerned about how much money they make not about social change.'

2. If you were starting a business what social or environmental campaign would you want to promote? Be ready to justify your answer to the class.

Many businesses now consider it important not only to make money but also to promote social and environmental change.

One company that has run ethical campaigns is The Body Shop which was started by Anita Roddick.

The Body Shop's mission statement begins: 'To dedicate our business to the pursuit of social and environmental change'. In the past twenty years there have been many campaigns in the stores to help communicate both national and international human rights and environmental issues.

▶ *Anita Roddick said, 'I want to work for a company that contributes to and is part of the community. I want something not just to invest in. I want something to believe in.'*

MADE WITH PASS!ON®

AGAINST	SUPPORT	ACTIVATE	DEFEND	PROTECT
ANIMAL	COMMUNITY	SELF	HUMAN	OUR
TESTING	TRADE	ESTEEM	RIGHTS	PLANET

Islam

When the lottery was introduced in Britain, many religions needed to consider what their response would be. Muslims must not charge interest on any type of loan as it exploits those in need. It is considered **haram** and against the rules of Allah. Receiving interest (**riba**) on money loaned is considered to be making the rich richer and causing hardship to others. Many Islamic banks now arrange for any interest gained to be sent directly to the customer's chosen charities.

Muslims are also against **qimar** (gambling) or any way of gaining money through chance. The Qur'an states:

'O you who believe! Intoxicants and games of chance … are only an uncleanness, the Shaitan's work; shun it therefore that you may be successful.'
(Surah 5:90)

▲ *The first Islamic bank was founded in 1975 and many exist throughout the world. In keeping with the Qur'an they neither charge interest on loans nor pay interest on deposits.*

Quakers

▲ *Many Quakers consider that important areas like health and the protection of the arts should be properly funded by the government and not rely on the lottery.*

Quakers (or Religious Society of Friends) are against gambling as they see it as gaining at the expense of others.

They believe it promotes the view that having lots of money can make people really happy. They also think that it promotes selfishness and goes against the Christian ethics of love, respect and concern for others.

Quakers are also concerned that the National Lottery gives grants to causes that they believe should be supported by public funding.

KEY WORDS

Riba   interest paid on money

Qimar   gambling

ACTIVITY THREE ••

1. Many workplaces run a weekly lottery syndicate. Nas (who is a Muslim) and Alice (who is a Quaker) have just started in their new office. It is Friday and Susan has come to ask if they want to join. Look at the information about Muslim and Quaker views on gaining wealth and copy and complete the **dialogue** below from either Nas's or Alice's point of view.

Susan Hi, I'm Susan. You're new to the office aren't you? Each Friday I collect the money for the lottery. Do you want to take part?

(YOUR) RESPONSE _____

Susan Is it for a religious or moral reason that you don't agree with the lottery?

(YOUR) RESPONSE _____

Susan I don't understand the harm you think it does. Could you explain it to me?

(YOUR) RESPONSE _____

Susan Thanks for explaining the reasons. It was really interesting. See you around sometime.

2. Find the correct tails to complete the heads below:

Quakers (Religious Society of Friends) ...

Muslims and Quakers both believe ...

For Muslims, gambling ...

... is considered haram and against the will of Allah.

... is a denomination of Christianity.

... it is wrong to take part in the lottery.

NOW TRY THIS ••••••••••••••••••••••••••••

The singer Sinead O'Connor said:

It's fine to make money. It isn't fine to make money your god.

1. Explain in your own words what you think she means.

2. Describe a situation when someone has made 'money their god'.

3. What about the earth's resources?

SKILLS

- **identifying** how humans are damaging the earth
- **thinking about** our own views on how we should care for the earth
- **producing** a lesson or presentation on how to treat the earth

ACTIVITY ONE

Below and opposite are two sets of pictures. Set A shows how humankind is damaging the earth and set B shows the effects or consequences of that damage. Decide which pictures from sets A and B go together and select the most suitable caption (a–d).

SET A: CAUSES

SET B: EFFECTS

5

6

8

7

a) *Pollution in rivers can kill plants and wildlife.*

b) *Deforestation destroys animal habitats and causes soil erosion.*

c) *Not feeding animals properly can result in mad cow disease or CJD.*

d) *Emissions of gases leads to the Greenhouse effect which can cause sea levels to rise.*

ACTIVITY TWO ●●●●●●●●●●●●●●●●●●●●●●●●●●●●●●●

In 1900 the world's population was one billion. In 2000 it was six billion.

1. The photo below shows one effect of this population increase. Suggest a caption for the photo which reflects the effect shown.

2. Based on what you have learned in this lesson so far, suggest other effects on the earth that might be caused by an increase in population.

These quotes show some people's attitudes to the earth's resources.

> Every living thing is sacred and is worthy of respect.

> All these floods and hurricanes show the earth is angry with the way she is being treated.

> All the time spent talking about the environment is not going to change anything.

> The land is God's gift. We inherit it from our parents and must leave it beautiful for our children.

> The planet was once beautiful but it's becoming more and more damaged. It's up to us all to save our world.

> The world has so many resources on offer – we can use all of these to make goods that people enjoy.

ACTIVITY THREE ....

Pick the two attitudes from the above you most agree with and the two you least agree with. Why have you picked these? Justify your selection to a partner.

NOW TRY THIS ....

Chief Seattle, the Chief of the Duwamish Native Americans, said:

> If we give you our Land, please teach your children what we have taught our children ... that the earth is our Mother.

You are the guardians of the earth for the next generation. How would you like to see children taught about how special the earth is and how it should be treated? Produce either a lesson or a PowerPoint® graphics presentation programme that could be used at a junior school.

You might want to consider the following:

- conserving energy and switching off lights
- recycling
- Fairtrade food
- dropping litter
- use of water.

▲ *Chief Seattle.*

4. What do religions say about care for the environment?

SKILLS

- **finding out** about Muslim and Christian attitudes to the earth
- **explaining and presenting** information

Why should people look after the earth's resources?

Well, I believe it is our duty to look after the earth, as it is a gift from God.

When God created the world he made humans to act as stewards and guard over the environment for the real owner.

It's not just ours to do what we like with or exploit.

Most Christians would say that not only did God create the world but he is still engaged in it.

I believe that Allah created and owns the world and that every human has a special role as **khalifah** to protect the environment. This is such an important responsibility that on the Day of Judgement Muslims will be asked by Allah how they have treated the earth and all living things.

The creation is finely balanced and to waste resources is to disobey Allah. Muslims make careful use of scarce resources such as water; hunting is allowed only for food and if a tree is cut down then another should be planted if possible.

When the Prophet Muhammad and his companions were on a long journey they stopped at a stream. His companions ran straight into the water and started to splash around in it. The Prophet, however, had taken a small bowl of water which he was washing with. They asked him why and he said, 'It was Allah who gave these gifts of water. He gave enough for us all but not to take more than we need.'

ACTIVITY ••

1. You have been asked to produce a booklet for Year 6 pupils to explain Christian and Muslim attitudes to the earth.

   These pages have a number of different sources to help you:

   • quotes from a Christian and a Muslim which explain their attitudes to the environment

   • some scripture quotes and religious teachings

   • a website address to collect further information or pictures.

   For your booklet you must include an explanation of:

   • the central beliefs of each religion using words and pictures to explain

   • the terms steward and khalifah

   • one quote for each religion and how it connects with Christian and Muslim attitudes.

   You can work in groups to produce the booklet.

2. Write down three questions you would ask a Muslim or Christian about their attitude to the environment.

3. Reread the quotations opposite about being a steward and khalifah and either design a poster or write a poem to show how you think people should care for the world.

Islam

'The earth is green and beautiful and Allah has appointed you His stewards over it.'

(Surah 6165)

'O children of Adam! ... eat and drink; but do not waste by being greedy, for Allah does not love wasters.'

(Surah 7:31)

'The central concept of Islam is **tawhid** or the unity of God. Allah is unity; and His unity is reflected in the unity of mankind and the unity of man and nature. His trustees are responsible for maintaining the unity of His creation, the integrity of the Earth, its flora and fauna, its wildlife and natural environment.'

(Islamic Declaration Assisi 1986)

Christianity

'Then the Lord God placed the man in the garden of Eden to cultivate it and guard it.'

(Genesis 2)

'In the beginning God created the heavens and the earth.'

(Genesis 1:1)

'The earth is the Lord's, and everything in it, the world, and all who live in it; for he founded it upon the seas and established it upon the waters.'

(Psalm 24:1–2)

Website

www.arcworld.org/faiths.htm

KEY WORDS

Caliph/Khalifah   agent or steward working for Allah

Tawhid   the oneness or unity of Allah

5. What attitudes do religious people have to animals?

SKILLS

- **identifying** different attitudes that humans have towards animals
- **analysing and comparing** how religious beliefs can inspire actions to care for animals
- **investigating** a range of sources to consider whether Jesus was a vegetarian

ACTIVITY ONE ••••••••••••••

1. With a partner copy and complete the concept map.

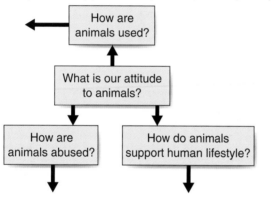

2. Is the life of a human being worth more than the life of a dog? Is it worth more than the life of 30 dogs? Discuss with a partner.

Sacred texts and teachings will affect the way many religious believers care for animals as well as humans.

Buddhism

'All breathing, existing, living sentient creatures should not be slain or treated with violence, nor abused, nor tormented, nor driven away.'

(Ahchoranga Sutra)

As a Buddhist monk I believe in reincarnation and believe in the past these may even have been my friends. The Temple is digging a deep moat to isolate twenty acres of forest and transform it to a tiger island.

◄ *Tigers are disappearing fast due to poachers. Abbot Acharn Phusit at Wat Pa Luangtabua Temple in Sai Yok offers sanctuary to wounded tigers and reintroduces their young to the wild. The first tiger arrived in 2000. It was ill and close to death.*

Hinduism

'No person should kill animals helpful to all. Rather by serving them one should attain happiness.'

(Bhagavad Gita)

In particular the Bhagavad Gita advises Hindus to protect and respect cows. Cows give milk like a natural mother and bulls plough the field producing grains and vegetables.

Many Hindus believe in **ahimsa** and so are vegetarians and will not harm animals. Krishna looked after his cows and is well known as Govinda (a herder of cows) because he worked with them, protected them and valued them.

Cows are allowed to roam free in India and since 1983 there has been a cow protection scheme at Bhaktivedanta Manor in England. Here they are well cared for. After the cows have been milked they are stroked.

Islam

'If someone kills a sparrow for sport, the sparrow will cry out on the Day of Judgement, "O Lord! That person killed me for nothing! He did not kill me for any useful purpose."'

(Hadith)

▶ *In 2000 the Muslim fishing communities pledged to conserve Misali Island in Tanzania, one of the most important turtle nesting sites which was under severe threat from dynamite fishing. Most of those who fish are Muslim and so, along with the Islamic Foundation for Ecology and Environmental Sciences and Muslim leaders in the area, they used the Qur'an and Shariah laws to come to a decision. One of the texts they used was Surah 7:31: 'O children of Adam! eat and drink; but waste not by excess for Allah loveth not the wasters.'*

ACTIVITY TWO ....

Complete the following table using information from each of the animal care projects described on these pages.

What are they doing?	Why are they doing it?	What are the religious principles involved?

Christianity

Although many religious people look at their sacred texts for guidance on how to live their lives, many issues are not directly mentioned in the texts. Therefore, people have to interpret the evidence from texts and religious teachings. One issue that many Christians discuss is: 'Was Jesus a vegetarian?'

What is the evidence?

▲ *An advertisement in America. What other ways can you think of for Christians to show respect for God's creation?*

ACTIVITY THREE ·············

1. From the evidence opposite (1–7), which do you think are the strongest and weakest arguments for Jesus being a vegetarian?

2. If Jesus was a vegetarian do you think all Christians should be? Be prepared to share your answer with the class.

Many different pieces of evidence are used to form a view:

1 In the Bible God says, 'Let us make man in our image, in our likeness, and let them rule over the fish of the sea and the birds of the air, over the livestock, over all the earth, and over all the creatures that move along the ground.' If people can rule over animals it means they can eat them.

2 In one of Jesus' teachings he said, 'Are not two sparrows sold for a penny? Yet not one of them will fall to the ground without the will of God.' If sparrows are so important, Jesus would not be eating any animals.

3 Animals are part of God's creation and the exploitation of them is against God's will.

4 Jesus did not eat the Passover lamb at the Last Supper.

5 If Jesus was a vegetarian why did he multiply fish at the feeding of the 5000?

6 Jesus threw the traders out of the temple because they were selling animals for sacrifice.

7 1 Timothy chapter 4 refers to food and says, 'Since everything God created is good, we should not reject any of it.'

NOW TRY THIS ....

The missionary Albert Schweitzer said, 'Compassion, in which all ethics must take root, can only attain its full breadth and depth if it embraces all living creatures and does not limit itself to humankind.'

Explain in your own words what this means.

KEY WORDS

Ahimsa   non-violence

Shariah   Islamic law

Sutra   a guideline

6. What makes us strong?

SKILLS

- **identifying** spiritual qualities
- **thinking about** your own spiritual qualities
- **finding out** how people look after their inner strength
- **reading about** Nkosi Johnson and identifying his inner strengths
- **using** your imagination to think about how your school could develop spiritual qualities

Labi Siffre wrote this song for the black community of South Africa during **apartheid**. It has been taken up as the anthem for victims of injustice throughout the world.

The higher you build your barriers
The taller I become
The farther you take my rights away
The faster I will run
You can deny me
You can decide to turn your face away
No matter, cos there's

Something inside so strong
I know that I can make it
Tho' you're doing me wrong, so wrong
You thought that my pride was gone
Oh no, something inside so strong.

▲ *In South Africa people were separated by race even when they were at the beach.*

◀ *White and black people lived separately with many black people living in appalling conditions.*

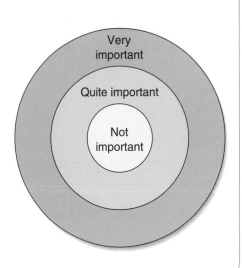

▶ *Protests against apartheid were often met by violence from the police.*

ACTIVITY ONE ....

1. Look at the pictures of apartheid and make a list of the rights that were taken away.

2. Think about all the people you have learned about in R.E. Choose one person for whom Labi Siffre's song could be an anthem and justify your choice to the class.

3. Copy the diagram to the right.

   Here is a list of inner strengths. Place each in the circle according to how you value them in your life.

   • self-control • patience • humility • gratitude • peace • love • gentleness • faith • hope • forgiveness • humanity • courage • perseverance (see Glossary) • goodness • truth • beauty • justice • freedom.

Very important

Quite important

Not important

Many people refer to the three different parts of themselves:

- *their mind*   • their body   • their **spirit**.

Just as people can take care of their mind and body, there are many ways to take care of their inner spirit or strength.

ACTIVITY TWO ....

Helen and Joe have made a table (below) of the ways they protect their mind and body but they are looking for different ways to look after their spirit. A number of people have given their personal views on what gives them a feeling of well-being. These are shown below. After you have read the views complete the table for Helen and Joe.

Mind	Body	Spirit
Reading	Going to the gym	?
Learning	Running marathons	
Doing quizzes	Football	
Su-doku	Healthy diet	
Using the computer	Cycling	
School	Swimming	

These extracts are from *My Well-being*.

'*Spend a little time laughing every day with someone you love.*'

(Kirsty Young, TV and radio presenter)

'*In a world that is often so dark and unsure we must look to each other, keep each other secure, to find our own light and to keep always bright needs God and his love and a sense of well-being.*'

(Lynda Bellingham, actress)

'*A smile from a stranger – the smell of the sea, a phone call from a loved one.*'

(Lesley Joseph, actress)

These extracts are from 'What Guides My Life', *Reader's Digest*.

'*There is a sort of atman (soul) that passes from life to life. And whatever that little spark is, your soul, that is the thing that endures. And that's the energy you feel when you love someone passionately; when you look at your child; when you're in the presence of a great piece of music or beautiful nature.*'

(Meera Syal, writer and actress)

'*I could never follow any religion, but I respect other people's. To me faith is like an inner strength and a belief in yourself – a belief in nature and the fact that we're all connected to it.*'

(Tracy Emin, artist)

Nkosi Johnson

Within every community there are people who have a strength of spirit that can inspire others. One such person was Nkosi Johnson.

Born in a township near Johannesburg, Nkosi never knew his father. He was one of 70,000 babies born in South Africa each year who are HIV positive. A worker at the hospital, Gail Johnson, took care of Nkosi when his mother became ill and died.

Gail fought for Nkosi to go to school when other parents opposed it because of the HIV virus. In July 2000 he spoke at an AIDS Conference about how important it is for people with AIDS to be accepted at school and within the community. Although he was only 11 and half the size he should have been, he talked to over 10,000 people. He pleaded for people to 'care for us and accept us – we are all human beings'. Nkosi died the following year.

▲ *Nkosi pleaded for people 'to care for us and accept us – we are all human beings'. Who else have you learned about who might make the same plea?*

ACTIVITY THREE ·············

1. What inner strengths do you think Nkosi showed?

2. One of the teachings in the Bible says:

   'Above all else, guard your inner strength, for it is the wellspring of life.'

   (Proverbs 4:23)

   Make a list of the ways that you 'guard your inner strength'. Compare them with your partner's list.

NOW TRY THIS ············

A survey has shown that although workers in the United Kingdom are among the most highly paid in the world, they are also among the most unhappy. Only 36 per cent of British employees enjoy their work. Some businesses are now giving opportunities for the spiritual development of their staff.

'It is finally being recognised that we need to appeal to employees' hearts and souls as well as to their minds and pockets.'

With a partner devise a plan to give opportunities for the spiritual development of pupils within your school.

KEY WORD

Spirit   of the inner being or soul

SUMMARY OF UNIT 4

Lesson 2

You have considered the impact on religious beliefs on ways of acquiring money and gambling.

Lesson 3

You have learned how humans are damaging the environment.

Lesson 1

You have learned about different religious attitudes to the importance of wealth.

What do religions say about the use of money and other resources?

Lesson 4

You have learned about Christian and Muslim attitudes to the environment.

Lesson 6

You have learned about different spiritual qualities.

Lesson 5

You have learned about Muslim, Buddhist and Hindu attitudes towards animal welfare.

UNIT 5: HOW DO BELIEFS AFFECT PEACE AND CONFLICT IN THE WORLD TODAY?

Lesson 1: Why are there conflicts?

◎ Distinguish between different types of conflict.

◎ Learn about different religious attitudes to conflict.

◎ Evaluate the idea of just war.

Lesson 2: Why are there different Christian attitudes to war?

◎ Read about different Christian views on war.

◎ Think about and forming your own opinion on whether Christians should take part in war.

◎ Investigate what the Bible says about war.

Lesson 3: How can peace be made and kept?

◎ Read about religious and non-religious ways of keeping the peace.

◎ Evaluate different methods of promoting peace.

◎ Find out about existing peace-keeping projects.

◎ Think about the importance of peace memorials.

Lesson 4: How can religions work together to create peace?

◎ Consider the nature of coexistence.

◎ Learn about Corrymeela, the Children of Abraham and the Interfaith Youth Council.

◎ Decide on the short- and long-term effects of peace projects.

Lesson 5: What attitudes do religions have to forgiveness?

◎ Learn about the Hand of Forgiveness Project and identify the impact of faith.

◎ Read teachings from the sacred texts concerning forgiveness.

◎ Learn about Sorry Sunday and Yom Kippur.

Lesson 6: When might conflict be necessary?

◎ Form your own opinion regarding human rights.

◎ Identify causes that you would make a stand for.

◎ Learn about the actions of Rosa Parks and consider her sources of inspiration.

◎ Read about Chiune Sugihara and identify his achievements.

How do beliefs affect peace and conflict in the world today?

1. Why are there conflicts?

SKILLS

- **identifying** different types of conflict
- **interpreting** teachings from religions about conflict and war
- **thinking about** what makes a war 'just'

Although all religions teach the importance of peace and love, nearly all of them have been or are involved in conflict. It might appear that religion is the cause of a conflict and that people are fighting in the name of God. This is because religion often has a large role to play in state affairs and so is a source of hostility between or within nations. Few conflicts are entirely religious in their cause.

ACTIVITY ONE •••••••••••••

In Unit 4 you learned about the importance of being at peace within oneself, yet so often we hear and see how conflict can occur within a person, between people, between communities and between countries.

1. You have five minutes to look through your textbook to find different examples of conflict.

2. Now compare your answers with a partner and group them into the following categories:

   a) examples of conflict between people

   b) examples of conflict between communities

   c) examples of conflict between countries.

◀ *An Israeli soldier who is also an Orthodox Jew.*

ACTIVITY TWO ....

1. Look at the photograph on the left. With a partner discuss whether anything surprises you about the image.

2. What clues show that the person in the picture is going to pray?

3. Suggest a suitable title for the picture. Justify your choice.

Each religion has its own general teachings on war and conflict, however, they all allow their followers to decide whether or not to get involved in either.

Christianity

Some Christians are **pacifists** and may refuse to take part in war. But the majority of Christians support the idea that violence is regrettable but sometimes necessary, based on the just war theory.

Just War

The conditions for the **just war** theory were first proposed by Thomas Aquinas who lived in the thirteenth century. They are:

a) to overcome evil

b) to be declared by the government

c) the last option – there is no other choice

d) it must be possible to win – it would be wrong to lose lives if there was no chance of winning

e) at the end the good must outweigh the loss of life it has caused

f) killing innocent people must be avoided.

ACTIVITY THREE ....

1. It is more than 700 years since the just war theory was formed. Things have changed. Imagine you have been given the opportunity to add two further rules to make a war a just war. From the list below, which would you choose? Be prepared to justify your answer to the class.

a) children must not be harmed

b) no child soldiers must be used

c) no people should be displaced from their countries

d) no use of nuclear bombs

e) civilians must not be bombed

f) animals must not be harmed

g) prisoners must be treated well

h) the war must not continue for more than three years

i) only the leaders of a country fight against each other.

2. Complete the following sentences, using the conditions for a just war on the left (a–f).

a) The condition I consider to be most important is … because …

b) The condition I consider to be the least important is … because …

▶ *Thomas Aquinas was an Italian Dominican monk who tried to define what would be a right intention for entering into a war.*

97

Buddhism

The first precept of Buddhism is non-harming and Buddhists try to resolve matters peacefully. There is no idea of a **holy war**. Many Buddhists are conscientious objectors and refuse to take part in wars even though they know they could be killed by their government for doing so.

The Buddhist code for monks allows them to defend themselves and they have been leaders in developing the Shaolin Order which is famed for its fighting skills.

'All tremble at violence; life is dear to all.

Putting oneself in the place of another, one should neither kill nor cause another to kill.'

(The Buddha, *Dhammapada*)

Humanism

Although there would be an individual response, most Humanists follow the **Golden Rule**: 'do as you would be done by'. Some are pacifists and others agree with the just war theory. Some Humanists are conscientious objectors and refuse to take part in any war.

Erasmus (a Christian humanist who lived in the sixteenth century) wrote about war:

'There is nothing more wicked, more disastrous, more widely destructive, more deeply tenacious, more loathsome, in a word, more unworthy of man.

Whoever heard of a hundred thousand animals rushing together to butcher each other, as men do everywhere?'

Islam

In Islam the principle of greater **jihad** is the struggle within oneself, while the lesser jihad refers to war and conflict between people. This is considered just if:

- it is in self-defence
- other nations have attacked an Islamic state
- another state is oppressing its own Muslims.

A holy war is allowed in defence of Islam. While revenge is condemned, self-defence is justified. Some Muslims are conscientious objectors and refuse to take part in war.

Sikhism

The Dharam Yudh (war in defence of righteousness) is similar to the rules in the just war theory apart from the view that a war should be undertaken even if it cannot be won.

Guru Nanak expressed the idea of a just war as:

'When all attempts to restore peace prove useless and no words avail,
Lawful is the flash of steel,
It is right to draw the sword.'

Some Sikhs are conscientious objectors and refuse to take part in war.

ACTIVITY FOUR

1. Read the religious teachings about war again on pages 97–99, then copy and complete the table.
2. In your table, highlight the similarities between the religions.

Religion	Teachings	Key Words	Example

NOW TRY THIS

St Cyprian said:

'If a murder is committed privately it is considered a crime. But if it happens with the authority of the state they call it courage.'

Are there any other things that happen in a war that would be considered a crime if the country was at peace?

KEY WORDS

Erasmus (1466–1536) Dutch Christian Humanist who became a priest in 1492

Golden Rule the rule that advises people to treat others in the same way as they would want to be treated themselves

Holy War war fought in defence of religion or religious teachings

Jihad every Muslim's individual struggle to resist evil in order to follow the path of Allah; also collective defence

Pacifism belief that all war is wrong

2. Why are there different Christian attitudes to war?

SKILLS

- **comparing** beliefs and practices of different denominations
- **thinking about** whether Christians should take part in wars
- **investigating** what the Bible says about wars

Within Christianity there are many denominations or religious groups. A denomination is formed when a group of Christians need to show that they are different from other Christians. This might be due to beliefs, practices or interpretations of teachings in the Bible. It is from these interpretations that members of denominations decide how they should live their lives and respond to modern-day issues.

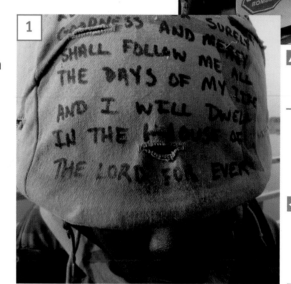

▲ *What clues are there in the picture to show these are Christians demonstrating against war?*

◄ *A soldier has written part of Psalm 23 on his helmet as he enters into war. Look up this passage in the Bible. Why do you think he has done this?*

ACTIVITY ONE ....

1. The pictures above show two different attitudes to war.

   a) What attitude to war does picture 1 show?

   b) What attitude to war does picture 2 show?

2. What do you think the people in pictures 1 and 2 would have considered before forming their attitudes? Choose from the list below.

   a) What does the Bible say?

   b) Is it God's will?

   c) What does the Church teach?

   d) Is the cause of the war justified?

   e) What do my friends and family think?

   f) What does my conscience say?

3. With a partner discuss what other issues you think different denominations might disagree on. You may want to consider:

   a) how you become a member of that denomination

   b) different forms of worship

   c) different beliefs about heaven

   d) different symbols in churches

   e) different views on divorce, abortion etc.

WHAT DO DIFFERENT DENOMINATIONS TEACH?

Below are various attitudes to war – although within denominations there are sometimes different views on issues of war and peace.

Baptists

Most Baptists believe war is the last resort if all methods of negotiation have failed. Peace-keeping is of first importance and this will come when there is justice on the earth.

Church of England

The Church of England has never condemned war and lives according to principles of the just war (see page 97). However, **indiscriminate** mass killing cannot be justified.

Jehovah Witnesses

Jehovah Witnesses are an example of the broader Christian family. Usually members refuse to fight in any war because they believe that it is wrong to take up weapons for an earthly government. During the Second World War many Jehovah Witnesses in Germany were put into concentration camps and died because they refused to join the Army.

Mennonites

This is a Church that grew out of the **Reformation** in Europe in the 1500s. Mennonites believe that Christ's command to 'love your enemies' stops them from participating in any military action.

Methodist Church

Methodists believe that war is contrary to the spirit and teaching of Jesus and peace-making is most important. Weapons of mass destruction are condemned and should never be used.

Quakers (Religious Society of Friends)

Quakers believe there is something of God in everyone and that more can be gained by appealing to the love and goodness in everyone.

Part of their Peace Testimony which was written in 1660 said: 'We utterly deny all outward wars and strife and fighting with outward weapons.'

ACTIVITY TWO

1. John has been asked to find out what the Amish believe about war. Make a list of ways in which he could research this.

2. Now look back to pages 46–47 and write a short description of the beliefs and practices of the Amish concerning war.

3. Draw a tree with two main branches or use the worksheet provided by your teacher.

   One branch should state: 'Will fight if attacked.'

   The other branch should state: 'Will not take part in a war.'

   From the main branches write the names of three denominations that believe in each statement.

4. Create a Venn diagram as shown below. Select any two denominations. Write one denomination in each of the outside circles. In the middle section write something the denominations agree on.

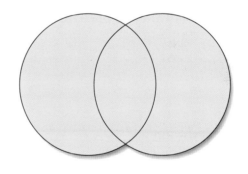

Roman Catholic

Usually Catholics uphold the beliefs of the just war. Some believe the only reason to use nuclear weapons is to prevent war.

ACTIVITY THREE ••••••••••••

1. For her RE homework, Amina has to answer the question:

   'Does the Bible teach that people should go to war?'

   She has collected a number of quotes and teachings from the Bible (1–12) but now has to divide them into 'yes' and 'no' groupings in answer to the question. After reading the information on these pages discuss with your partner which you would put in each category.

2. On your own write 50 words to show how you think Amina should answer the question. When you have finished swap your answer with your partner and see if you can agree on an answer.

4 Jesus spoke about 'turning the other cheek'.

5 In the Sermon on the Mount, Jesus taught that people should work for peace.

6 The Bible teaches that people should fight against evil.

7 In the Bible there are references to war 'Proclaim this among the nations; prepare for war' (*Joel 3:9*).

1 In *Romans 13*, Paul wrote that God has placed our ruling authorities in power and therefore Christians should obey them if they tell people to go to war.

8 Jesus became angry when people were misusing the Temple: 'He overturned the tables of the money-changers and the benches of those selling doves' (*Mark 11:15*).

2 Jesus did not condemn the centurion (*Luke 7:1–10*) for being part of the military.

3 There is something of God in everyone.

▲ *A Quaker group's piece of* **The Peace Ribbon***, which stretched for fifteen miles. How would you get your message across?*

9
In *Matthew 5:9* it says: 'Blessed are the peacemakers.'

10
In *Matthew 5:44* it says: 'Love your enemies, and pray for those who **persecute** you.'

11
When Jesus was being arrested he said: 'Put your sword back in its place for all those who draw the sword will die by the sword' (*Matthew 26:52*).

12
In the Ten Commandments (in *Exodus 20:13*) it says: 'Do not kill.'

▲ *There are many areas of conflict in the world today. What are the short-term and the long-term effects of war?*

▲ *Coventry Cathedral 'Reconciliation'. This sculpture by Josefina De Vasconcellos stands in the ruins of the old cathedral which was bombed in World War II. It was given by Richard Branson as a token of reconciliation. An identical sculpture is in the Peace Garden in Hiroshima, Japan.*

NOW TRY THIS ············

Write a reply to the following statement:

'All Christians believe in war.'

In your response you should include the following words: stereotype; denominations; conscience; pacifists; just war.

KEY WORD

Reformation religious movement in the sixteenth century to reform the Roman Catholic Church which led to the formation of the Protestant Churches

3. How can peace be made and kept?

SKILLS

• **recognising** the difference between keeping and making peace
• **finding out** about peace-keeping projects
• **comparing and deciding** about strategies for keeping peace
• **thinking about** the importance of peace memorials

ACTIVITY ONE

1. Look at the cartoon sequence then discuss the question below in groups. Be ready to share your answers with the rest of the class.

   'At the beginning of the day two people were in conflict but by the end of the day how many people would need to make peace with others?'

2. What do you think is the difference between keeping peace and making peace?

Helen finds her favourite shirt isn't ironed – shouts at mum.

Mum goes to start breakfast and finds there is no milk – shouts at husband and son.

Husband goes to school – shouts at his class.

Children in his class go home in bad moods – shout at home.

ACTIVITY TWO ● ● ● ● ● ● ● ● ● ● ●

The community you live in has many different nationalities and religions. You have been awarded a grant to fund a project for the community to work together.

The criteria are:

1. The project has been used before elsewhere and has been successful.

2. It will include a lot of people from the community.

3. It will have a lasting effect.

The following four projects have made it through to the final stage. Now you and your partners have to select one and justify your selection.

You will then have to present your selection to the rest of the class ready for a class vote.

Project One – Music

A band will form reflecting the diversity of the community. The band will play at many community concerts. This project is based upon the work of Ibrahim Bangura who lives in Sierra Leone, the poorest country in Africa, which has had a long civil war. Bangura writes songs about tolerance and peace. He is trying to help former child soldiers to return to live within their countries without discrimination.

▲ *Children need to be helped in many ways once they have been child soldiers. This former child soldier was drugged and forced to commit atrocities during the ten-year civil war in Sierra Leone.*

Project Two – Peace sit-ins

If Peace cannot be Maintained with honour It is no longer Peace

PEACE AND SILENCE IS MUST FOR NATION.

◄ *Indian Kashmiri students use a sit-in to protest for peace in Srinagar, 9th October 2004. More than 2000 students from various leading schools participated.*

Every Saturday members of the community will sit in the shopping centre dressed in white and have a silent sit-in to protest against violence. This project is based on the students' protest in India which called for people to stop using violence in politics.

Project Three – Peace art

All members of the community will work together to paint pictures and messages about the importance of peace. This idea is based upon the Art Miles Mural Project, which now exists in over 100 countries. People work together to design and paint a mural on an issue they have concerns about, e.g. role of women or the environment.

Project Four – Paper birds of peace

The peace crane is now used as a global symbol for peace. Many have been placed in the church next to the Twin Towers Memorial site. Can you find another picture of the peace crane in this unit?

This project will create thousands of paper cranes with a message of peace that will be displayed in schools, community centres, hospitals, places of worship and leisure centres. It is based upon the work of Sadako who contracted leukaemia after the US atomic bombing of her home in Hiroshima, Japan in 1945. She promised to fold 1000 paper cranes saying: 'Paper crane, I will write peace on your wings and you will fly all over the world.' She made 644 before she died at the age of 12. After her death the community worked together to complete the rest and the paper crane has since become a symbol of world peace.

NOW TRY THIS ....

'Every town that has a war memorial should also have a memorial showing the importance of keeping peace.'

Write down why you agree or disagree with this statement.

4. How can religions work together to create peace?

SKILLS

- **interpreting** pictures to suggest meanings
- **thinking about** different ways of achieving harmony and co-existence
- **finding out** about different religious projects aimed at creating peace
- **describing** the short- and long-term effects of peace projects

Throughout the world there are people of different religions who find it difficult to **co-exist**. This may be a result of arguments over land, money or past events.

Many religious and non-religious groups organise projects to help different religions work together in harmony.

ACTIVITY ONE

Look at the picture below for two minutes. Your teacher will be timing you.

Now close your book. The teacher will ask you three questions:

1. Which religions do you think the picture is referring to?
2. How do you know?
3. Where do you think this picture was taken?

▲ *A plea for people of different faiths to live together in harmony.*

In Year 7 you may have learned about the following places where people have not lived together peacefully in the past.

Often in areas of conflict religions will try to work together to produce harmony.

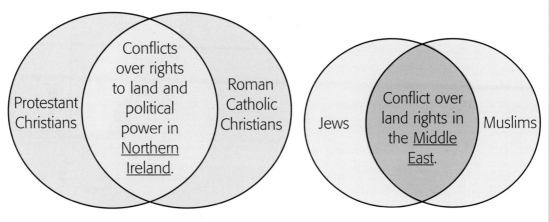

Protestant Christians — Conflicts over rights to land and political power in <u>Northern Ireland</u>. — Roman Catholic Christians

Jews — Conflict over land rights in the <u>Middle East</u>. — Muslims

Corrymeela Project

Corrymeela (this means 'Hill of Harmony') supports Protestants and Catholics in Northern Ireland by providing opportunities for meetings and dialogue to try to stop prejudice and fear of each other.

Many projects involve working with young children, for example the creation of the Peace Wall. In Belfast, large walls keep Catholic and Protestant neighbours apart. Often the children would throw bricks over the wall at each other. People from Catholic and Protestant groups met to consider what they could do. They ran a children's programme where a clown made the children realise the hurt of being laughed at because of being different.

The Protestant and Catholic children went away together and some became best friends. Eventually they agreed to stop throwing stones.

The person who led the programme passed through the area a few days later. She saw the children hanging around on opposite sides of the wall and asked what they were doing. They said they waited there every day on their way back from school so they could shout hello to their friends.

CORRYMEELA IS PEOPLE OF ALL AGES AND CHRISTIAN TRADITIONS, WHO, INDIVIDUALLY AND TOGETHER ARE COMMITTED TO THE HEALING OF SOCIAL, RELIGIOUS & POLITICAL DIVISIONS THAT EXIST IN NORTHERN IRELAND AND THROUGHOUT THE WORLD

◀ *Corrymeela is a Christian Community that aims to heal the social, religious and political divisions that exist in Northern Ireland and throughout the world.*

Children of Abraham Project

Children of Abraham was started by a Jewish man and a Muslim woman who decided their communities knew little about each other. The name reflects the idea that Jews and Muslims share a common spiritual ancestor, the Biblical **patriarch** Abraham. It hopes to build an understanding between Muslims and Jews worldwide through the Internet. Each week different photos of Muslim and Jewish life are explained so that people can understand the different beliefs and practices.

▲ *Through the activities of Children Of Abraham young people learn about each other's religions and cultures. Which Jewish festival is she learning about? Reading page 60 may help.*

The project is web-based and has chat rooms to encourage dialogue between the two faiths. When children use the chat rooms they find that they have much more in common than they have differences. Unlike other interfaith efforts that stress only the similarities, Children of Abraham allows the participants to engage in frank discussions about subjects such as suicide bombings by Palestinians and Israel's military occupation of the West Bank and Gaza.

Nadia Sheikh is a member of Children of Abraham and she said: 'It's something you feel you have to do. You are not only spreading peace and knowledge, you are getting a better understanding. There isn't the possibility you could have a closed mind ever again.'

ACTIVITY TWO ....●●●

1. The two projects described so far in this lesson have had a number of short- and long-term effects. Copy the diagram for each project or use the worksheet provided. In the centre write the title of the project. Under the 'Action' heading write two things the project does and then describe what you think may be the long- and short-term effects.

2. Underneath each diagram draw possible logos for each project and explain how it represents the work of the project.

3. Discuss with your partner why you think the two projects are called Hill of Harmony and Children of Abraham.

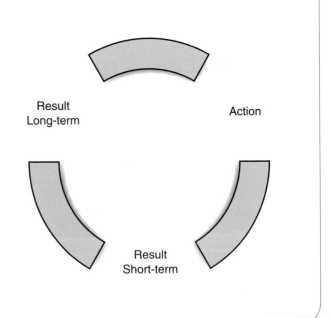

Result
Long-term

Action

Result
Short-term

Liverpool Interfaith Youth Council Project

The Liverpool Interfaith Youth Council unites people aged fourteen to nineteen from different faith backgrounds.

Its aim is:

- to promote understanding, respect and positive co-operation
- to encourage the teenagers to work together to make decisions about their community
- to develop active citizenship within the local community
- to develop self-confidence and increase understanding of those with beliefs different from their own.

ACTIVITY THREE ....

1. Below are some pictures showing the youth council at work. If you had to choose a picture to show each of their aims which would you choose?

   Now write a caption for each, which shows the aim(s) and also how they put it into practice.

2. How would you reply to someone who says: 'It is the adults who should learn to make peace. Getting teenagers to work together is just a waste of time?'

   In your answer you need to include two reasons to justify your view.

▲ *A Hindu dance workshop.*

▲ *A youth camp.*

◀ *Discussions at a conference.*

NOW TRY THIS ....

What do you think Nadia meant when she said:

'There isn't the possibility you could ever have a closed mind again.' (Page 110.)

Why do you think people might have a 'closed mind'?

5. What attitudes do religions have to forgiveness?

SKILLS

• **thinking** about the power of forgiving
• **considering** the impact of beliefs upon forgiveness
• **finding out** about the importance of Yom Kippur for many Jews

ACTIVITY ONE

Researchers have found that giving up grudges and revenge may have healing powers such as reducing bad back pain, helping stop drug and alcohol abuse and generally improving people's health.

Discuss with a partner why you think this might happen.

The Hand of Forgiveness

▲ *Tariq, a twenty-year-old student, who was shot while delivering pizzas.*

◄ *His killer Tony Hicks was fourteen and received a 25-year prison sentence.*

▼ *Azim Khamisa, Tariq's father.*

> When I got the phone call saying Tariq was dead it was like a nuclear bomb going off in my heart. There was no solace to be found and I turned to my faith as a Sufi Muslim. For the next few days I survived through prayer and was quickly given the blessing of **forgiveness**, reaching the conclusion that there were victims at both ends of the gun ...
>
> In my faith on the fortieth day after a death you are encouraged to channel your grief into good compassionate deeds ... I reached out to Ples Felix, the grandfather and guardian of Tony ... We are very different but we share a common purpose.
>
> Five years after the tragedy I met Tony. It was a very healing time. I found him very likeable, well mannered and sorry. I told him when he got out of prison there would be a job waiting for him at the Tariq Khamisa Foundation.
>
> You forgive for yourself, because it moves you on. I have recently written a letter asking for a lesser sentence for Tony.

(Abridged from the Tariq Khamisa Foundation website.)

▼ *Ples Felix, Tony's grandfather and guardian.*

Tony is my daughter's only child and he grew up in the violent streets of Los Angeles. When he was eight he saw the murder of his cousin and became involved with older boys.

The night before the shooting I told him he wouldn't be able to go out if he didn't do his homework. He ran away. Two days later I got a phone call from the police saying, 'Mr Felix, your grandson is no longer considered a runaway. He is now the prime suspect in a murder inquiry.' I felt anger, shame and loss. I also felt guilt as I was his guardian. He tried to keep up a false bravado but then he broke down and cried and said how sorry he was.

When the three of us met in prison it was probably hardest for Azim. When Azim left, Tony said, 'That is a very special man. I shot and killed his only son and yet he can sit with me, encourage me, and then offer me a job.'

Together Ples Felix and Azim Khamisa established the Tariq Khamisa Foundation which visits schools and inspires students to say no to gangs, guns and violence. It aims to develop a culture of peacemakers. It has reached over eight million students in 12,000 schools.

ACTIVITY TWO ··

1. Negative and positive emotions are often considered as two sides of the same coin.

   Read the stories again and decide how Tony, Azim or Ples changed one feeling (a–f) into the other.

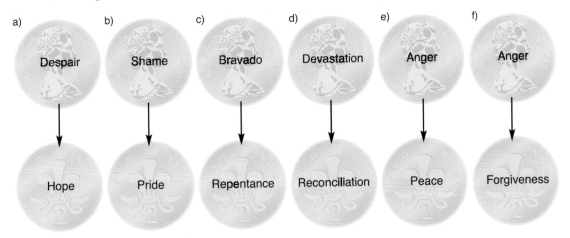

a) Despair → Hope
b) Shame → Pride
c) Bravado → Repentance
d) Devastation → Reconciliation
e) Anger → Peace
f) Anger → Forgiveness

2. Discuss with your partner how you think Azim's faith may have helped him. Be ready to justify your answers to the class.

ACTIVITY THREE ···········

All religions believe that forgiveness is important and that it is important to offer the hand of forgiveness even if you feel you have been wronged.

Read the quotes from the different religions below. Draw round one of your hands and in each of the fingers write what someone should do to show their forgiveness.

Christianity

'Peter asked Jesus, "Master, how many times should I forgive my brother if he continues to wrong me? Is seven times enough?" Jesus said to him, "No. Not seven times, but seventy times seven."'

(Matthew 18:21)

Hinduism

'A superior being does not render evil for evil.'

(Ramayana-Yuddha Kanda 115)

Islam

'The best deed of a great man is to forgive and forget.'

(Nahjul Balagha, Saying 201)

Judaism

'Who is the bravest hero? He who turns his enemy into a friend.'

(Nathan 23)

Sikhism

*'Those who beat you with fists,
Do not pay them in the same coin,
But go to their house and kiss their feet.'*

(Adi Granth, Shalok, Farid)

Taoism

*'After an attempt at reconciliation, if bitterness still remains — what then?
Meet bitterness with kindness.'*

(Tao Te Ching 79)

It is often difficult to know when to say sorry. Sometimes people have small disagreements and neither will be the first to apologise. Many religious traditions teach the importance of believers taking that first step in **reconciliation**.

New Year Greetings
FROM BOTH OF US

▲ *Many Jews believe they are judged during Rosh Hashanah, with the names of the people who are good written in the Book of Life. The shofar, or ram's horn, is blown during synagogue services to call people to repent.*

Christians are taught that being sorry for their sins and asking for God's forgiveness are an important part of life. In reciting the Lord's Prayer they say, 'Forgive us our sins as we forgive those who sin against us.'

Some Christian churches hold a Say Sorry Sunday near National Forgiveness Day on 30 September. Its aim is to stop the cycle of conflict, violence and crime.

For Jews the sense of being forgiven is part of the relationship with God. The process begins with **Teshuvah – repentance** – which many see as the turning point in someone's life.

In order to repent they try to see how they can make amends for what they have done wrong, for example, a thief giving back the goods. The next step is to confess the sins before God. This happens at **Yom Kippur**, which is ten days of penitence that begins at **Rosh Hashanah**.

'For forgiveness between a person and God, Yom Kippur can atone; for sins between a person and his or her fellow human being, Yom Kippur cannot atone, until he or she makes peace with his or her fellow human being.'

(Mishnah Yoma 8:9)

NOW TRY THIS ....

The question you have been asked is:

'Where might religious people get guidance and support to be able to forgive?'

You have ten minutes with your partner to devise a concept map to answer the question. Spend the first two minutes skim reading all the information again in this lesson.

KEY WORDS

Forgive to stop being angry with someone

Reconciliation making up or reaching an agreement and working together again

Rosh Hashanah Jewish New Year which is celebrated in the autumn

Teshuvah repentance

Yom Kippur Day of Atonement. A fast day which occurs ten days after Rosh Hashanah

6. When might conflict be necessary?

SKILLS
- **discussing** how responsible we should be for protecting human rights
- **thinking about** what you might take a moral stand for
- **analysing** the impact of Rosa Parks's and Chiune Sugihara's beliefs on their actions

BRANDON Are you going to the demonstration march?

LEAH No! What's the point? No one will take any notice of demonstrations. Anyway the new law doesn't affect us. We're not that religion.

BRANDON Of course it affects us. We're human aren't we? Shouldn't we try to treat others as we want to be treated?

LEAH I don't know what you are so worked up about.

BRANDON Just think about what we learned in R.E. about how the Jews were treated in the **Holocaust**. About how many people stood by when people were being persecuted.

LEAH Yes, but the people who practise that religion, they're not like us … I mean those clothes they wear draw attention to the fact that they are different. And they always seem to stick together.

BRANDON The clothes have a special meaning for the traditions. It's a bit sad if we feel we need to **persecute** people because of what they wear. Bit of a worry for football fans!

It isn't right to fight

You said, 'It isn't right to fight'

But when we watched the news tonight

You shook your fist and said

You wished the tyrant and his **cronies** dead.

When I asked why,

If it's not right to fight,

You gave a sigh.

You shook your head

And sadly said,

'Sometimes a cause is just,

And if there is no other way,

Perhaps you must'.

(By John Foster, from *Standing on the Sidelines*)

ACTIVITY ONE •••••••••••••••

1. Look at the dialogue and poem above. Make a list of the reasons that are given for standing up for the rights of others.

2. With a partner look through a local and a national newspaper and select one issue from each that you both feel strongly about. Then put the following (a–d) in order of effectiveness to let people know your feelings. Be ready to justify your answer.

   a) Write a letter to your local council stating your views.

   b) Organise a petition.

   c) Pray that it will change.

   d) Talk to your friends about the situation.

Throughout history many people have felt that their human rights have been taken away by people who are in power. Some remain quiet in the hope that they won't be noticed but others put their lives at risk by protesting.

▶ *Rosa Parks being fingerprinted after her arrest.*

Rosa Parks

One such person is Rosa Parks. Rosa lived in Montgomery, Alabama, at the time of Martin Luther King. There were strict laws of segregation then, which did not allow white and black people to mix in public places.

Rosa changed the course of history on 1 December 1955 when she refused to give up her seat to a white passenger on a bus.

◀ *In Alabama white and black people were not allowed to mix in public places. Who else have you learned about who also campaigned against this segregation?*

Rosa Parks said, 'I know someone had to take the first step and I made up my mind not to move.'

ACTIVITY TWO

1. Work in small groups. Imagine you have been asked to produce a short film about the life of Rosa Parks. Decide which three scenes you would include. Use the comic strip above and websites that will be given to you by your teacher as sources of information.

   Decide which characters will be included. Plan your film as a flow diagram. Be sure to show why Rosa decided to take the action she did.

2. Because of Rosa Parks's actions she was known as 'the Mother of the Modern Day Civil Rights Movement'. She ran 'The Parks **Legacy**' which teaches young people about important issues that affect the future of the world.

   Select three issues that you think should be taught.

Chiune and Yukiko Sugihara

The following is a student's response to an assignment.

▶ *Chiune and Yukiko Sugihara.*

For my assignment I am going to write about Chiune and Yukiko Sugihara.

Chiune was the Japanese Consul-General in 1939 in Lithuania. After Hitler's invasion of Poland many Jews escaped to Lithuania – fleeing from the Holocaust. When Lithuania was also invaded it was too late for most Jews to be able to escape.

In July 1940 all the consuls were told to leave the country but Chiune asked for a twenty-day extension. On a morning in late July 1940 Consul Sugihara woke to find lots of Jews outside the Japanese Consulate. They had realised the only way out of the country was to get visas to go east. Sugihara didn't have the authority to issue so many visas so he asked his Japanese government three times if he could give out more. Each time he was refused with the final notice saying:

CONCERNING TRANSIT VISAS REQUESTED PREVIOUSLY I ADVISE ABSOLUTELY NOT TO BE ISSUED … NO EXCEPTIONS … NO FURTHER ENQUIRIES EXPECTED.

Chiune knew he should obey his country but he also knew he had to follow his conscience. So for 29 days he and his wife endlessly wrote and signed visas by hand – more than 300 a day. Chiune didn't have to help – after all he wasn't Jewish. When he went back to Japan in 1947, he was asked to resign from the foreign service and lost his rights to a pension because he had disobeyed orders by issuing the visas.

When he was asked why he did it he said, 'I'm glad I found the strength to make the decision to save them. They were human beings and so I had to help them. I may have disobeyed my country but if I didn't I would have been disobeying my God.'

Today there are 40,000 descendents from the survivors of Sugihara who owe their lives to him. One man who gave life to 40,000 people.

The reason why I chose Chiune is because although I am only fourteen I owe my life to Chiune and his wife because if he hadn't given my great-grandfather his visa I would not have been born.

▶ *Many visitors go to the office where Sugihara worked in Lithuania. Why do you think they put paper cranes on the desk he issued visas from?*

118

▲ *Holocaust survivor Hanni Vogelweid poses near a memorial dedicated to Chiune Sugihara, after it was unveiled at the Museum of Tolerance in Los Angeles. Vogelweid and her family were helped by the Sugiharas, who disobeyed orders from Tokyo about issuing exit visas to Jews.*

ACTIVITY THREE ••••••••••

1. The information opposite was written by a fourteen-year-old pupil. What do you think was the title that the teacher had set for the assignment?

2. If you were going to interview Chiune Sugihara what five questions would you want to ask him?

3. Many visitors go to Lithuania each year to visit his office. Why do you think peace cranes are placed on his desk? (Look back to page 107.)

4. Chiune was given an award by Yad Vashem, the Holocaust Museum in Israel and a park has been named after him.

   If you had to write a description to go on the plate outside the park, what would you write?

   You can use a maximum of eleven words to finish it off but it must begin with the words, 'This park is dedicated to Chiune Sugihara, a man who …'.

NOW TRY THIS ••••••••••

Create a Venn diagram to show the differences and similarities between the actions and motivations of Rosa Parks and Chiune Sugihara.

KEY WORD

Holocaust   also known as The Shoah. Suffering experiences and persecution of European Jews by the Nazis

SUMMARY OF UNIT 5

Lesson 2

You have learned about different Christian attitudes to war.

Lesson 3

You have learned that there are different religious and non-religious ways of trying to make and keep peace.

Lesson 1

You have learned that there are different types of conflict and what is meant by a just war.

How do beliefs affect peace and conflict in the world today?

Lesson 4

You have learned how Corrymeela and Children of Abraham promote peace between and within religions.

Lesson 6

You have learned that many people consider it important to take a stand for human rights.

Lesson 5

You have learned that most religions consider forgiveness as important in making and keeping peace.

Glossary

Adhan   the call to prayer in Islam

Ahimsa   non-violence

Amnesty International   voluntary organisation working for human rights around the world

Anti-Semitism   hostility to or against Jews

Apartheid   policy that happened in South Africa keeping different people apart

Arjuna   third son of King Pandu. He heard the Bhagavad Gita from Krishna

Awe   filled with wonder

Baha'u'llah   (1817–1892) founder of the Bahai's

Caliph/Khalifah   agent or steward working for Allah

Chastity   not having sex until after marriage

Civil war   war between people of the same country

Co-existence   living together peacefully

Community   a group living in one place or having common interests

Concept map   a diagram intended to explain a concept or thought

Confess   to admit you have done something wrong

Conflict   disagreements

Conscience   a person's sense of what is right and wrong

Conscientious Objector   a person who refuses to do military service because of their religious or moral beliefs

Contemplative   a person who practices spiritual or religious meditation

Convent   a community of nuns

Cronies   mates, friends

Day of Judgement   when God makes his final decision on how a person has acted during their life

Deforestation   stripping of trees from an area

Deities   gods

Dialogue   an attempt to build bridges of communication with another person

Discrimination   making an unfair distinction in the way you treat other people

Diva   candle in Hinduism

Dynamite fishing   fishing with explosives

Erasmus   (1466–1536) Dutch Christian Humanist who became a priest in 1492

Ethics   the study of what is right and wrong

Faith   complete trust or confidence

Forgive   to stop being angry with someone

Free will   the belief that everyone is responsible for their own actions and that nothing is determined in life

Ghee   clarified butter

Golden Rule   the rule that advises people to treat others in the same way as they would want to be treated themselves

Greenhouse effect   sunlight coming in but the heat not escaping

Gurdwara   the Sikh place of worship

Guru   in Sikhism it is used to refer to one of the ten historic leaders of the community and also of God

Hadith   stories about or sayings of the Prophet Muhammad

Hafiz   title given to Muslims who learn the whole of the Qur'an by heart

Hanukkah/Chanukah   Jewish festival of lights

Haram   in Islam, anything that is unlawful or not permitted

Harmony   in agreement

Heaven   where God is found to his full extent

Hell   where God is absent

Hijab modest dress worn by many Muslim women to cover their hair and bodies

Holocaust also known as the Shoah. Suffering experiences of European Jews by the Nazis

Holy War war fought in defence of religion or religious teachings

Humility being modest or humble

Ibrahim (Abraham) one of the five main prophets of Islam

Identity all the different aspects that make a human being unique

Id-ul-Fitr Muslim festival marking the end of Ramadan, the month of fasting

Immoral what is wrong

Impact strong influence or effect

Indiscriminate including everyone or everything

Indra Hindu deity in charge of rain

Integrate to bring together people or groups

Islamaphobia irrational fear or dislike of Muslims

Janmashtami the festival celebrating Krishna's birth

Jihad every Muslim's individual struggle to resist evil in order to follow the path of Allah; also collective defence

Just War a theory which outlines the conditions necessary for it to be right to go to war

Kaliya a giant river serpent

Karma Hindu and Buddhist principle that determines the consequence of one life for another

Kiddush a prayer usually recited over wine at Shabbat and other festivals

Kosher foods or practices that are allowed for Jews

Krishna one of the most popular of the Hindu gods who came to earth in human form

Labi Siffre a black, British songwriter

Legacy something that you want to pass onto the next generation

Maghrib prayer compulsory daytime prayer for Muslims

Materialistic concerned with the importance of money

Maya an illusion in Hinduism

Moksha release or liberation. Usually used to refer to becoming free from the cycle of birth and death

Monastery a community of monks

Moral what is right

Moral evil evil events that happen due to the power of humans

Mosque the Muslim place of worship

Natural evil evil events that happen due to the power of nature

Ner Tamid eternal light found in synagogues

Obedience to do as commanded or requested

Orthodox Judaism a form of Judaism believing in the traditional teachings of the religion

Pacifism belief that all war is wrong

Patriarch a ruler of family or tribe

Persecute to be continually cruel

Persevere to carry on despite difficulties

Poverty having little or no money, resources and possessions

Prejudice an unfair opinion that is not based on reason or experience

Qimar the Muslim word for gambling

Quakers (Society of Friends) a community of Christians founded by George Fox in the seventeenth century

Reconciliation making up or reaching an agreement and working together again

Reformation religious movement in the sixteenth century to reform the Roman Catholic Church which led to the formation of the Protestant Churches

Reform Judaism a form of Judaism believing that all the old laws of Judaism do not have to be followed exactly

Reincarnation a belief that human beings are born into new lives in this world after they die
Repent to be sorry for what you have done
Retreat a place which is quiet and peaceful and allows people to think
Reverence a feeling of deep respect and awe
Revert to decide to follow a different faith
Riba in Islam, interest on money borrowed or lent
Right something someone is entitled to
Ritual a ceremony or pattern of actions used in religious worship
Role model someone who possesses inspirational characteristics
Rosh Hashanah Jewish New Year which is celebrated in the autumn

Sacred dedicated to a god or holy purpose
Sacrifice giving up something valued for someone or something else
Samsara cycle of birth, death and rebirth
Secular Jew Jews who do not normally consider religion as important but have been born of a Jewish mother or converted to Judaism
Segregate to separate people or groups from each other
Service the act of helping
Shabbat Jewish holy day (Sabbath) beginning at Friday sunset and ending on Saturday at nightfall
Shariah Islamic law
Sit-in a form of protest where people refuse to move
Society of Friends (Quakers) a community of Christians founded by George Fox in the seventeenth century
Soil erosion removal of topsoil by wind and rain
Spirit of the inner being or soul
Stereotype a person or thing considered to represent a group
Steward to look after and care for the world. Many Christians believe this is a God-given responsibility
Sufi a Muslim who tries to give up materialistic life and concentrates on the spiritual journey towards Allah
Sutra a guideline in Buddhism

Symbol something that represents or suggests something else

Tawhid the oneness or unity of Allah
Teshuvah repentance in Judaism
The Rule guidance of particular Christian monasteries
Torah the Jewish holy scripture
Tradition the passing down of customs and beliefs from one generation to the next
Transitory moving, changing

Ummah the worldwide community of Muslims

Vegetarian someone who does not eat meat and often refuses to wear leather
Vocation a sense of commitment or calling for a career or occupation
Vows promises
Vrindavan centre of pilgrimages in India. Where Krishna lived

Wonder to have a feeling of admiration

Yom Kippur Day of Atonement. A fast day which occurs ten days after Rosh Hashanah